PRAISE FO

"Paul Yin brought me and thousands others into the Employee Assistance field which is benefitting millions. His energy, charisma, dedication, humor, and love for humanity is contagious. This book should be required reading for everyone in the EAP field . . . [and] everyone in psychology, education, and every field that works with people. My highest recommendations!"

> ~*Dr. Tan Peifang*, Board of Directors, *China Employee Assistance Professional Association*

"*Explosions of Joy* is an extraordinary tribute to counselor Paul Yin and to grieving families of Malaysia Flight 370 disaster . . . Especially poignant are details of Paul's insightful ability to reach beyond traditional counseling, to help families in their darkest hours . . . Discover joy and be spellbound in its wake."

> ~*Ellen Weber (PhD), Mita International Brain Center*

"A brilliant, haunting, and healing book . . . [Paul's] personal sharing and humor make it come alive!"

> ~*Dr. Herb Goldberg*, author of *What Men Still Don't Know About Women, Relationships, and Love; The Hazards of Being Male: Surviving the Myth of Masculine Privilege; Creative Aggression*, and several others

"Like the chaplains of 9/11 who held others and myself up, Paul sacrifices of himself to sit with those experiencing incredible pain in tragedy. His willingness to share his wisdom both teaches and inspires all who have the honor to read his words."

> ~Paul F. Bauer, Retired Police Lieutenant, Licensed Professional Counselor, and author of *40 Days in the Desert: A Devotional Guide for Uniform Services Personnel*

Explosions of Joy

A Memoir of the Grief Counselor for Missing Malaysia Airlines Flight 370

By Paul Yin with Trina A. Kraus

Kraus House Publishing

Pennsylvania, U.S.A.

Contributing Editor: Ken Rutt
Cover Design by Ken Raney
Photograph by Stefani Schweiger

"A Generation" by Gu Cheng, translated by Joseph R. Allen, from SEA OF DREAMS, copyright ©1979 by Gu Cheng, translation ©2005 by Joseph R. Allen. Reprinted by permission of New Directions Publishing Corp.

ISBN: 978-0-692-06573-0
ISBN: 978-0-692-06574-7 (e)

Printed in the United States of America

Published by Kraus House Publishing, LLC
Pennsylvania

Some names and identifying details have been changed to protect the privacy of those involved, and some events have been slightly modified for clarity.

DEDICATION

To my loving parents, my always supportive wife Vanessa, my miracle baby Kimi, my grandmother and sister Sherry up in heaven, and everyone whom I had the privilege to encounter on this unique path. ~Paul Yin

To John, to my daughters Eden and Lily, my family, my dear friend Brian, and all of my students. ~Trina A. Kraus

ACKNOWLEDGEMENTS

The authors wish to acknowledge the deep ineffable loss experienced by all involved in the tragedies mentioned herein and thank those who were willing to share their stories.

In addition, the authors also wish to thank those who have supported the creation of this text, especially Ken Rutt, whose unwavering enthusiasm and divergent thinking formed an improbable union between two authors. Paul Yin also wishes to thank the "visa officer" wherever he may be, and hopes that Yu (Rudy) Qingchuan will one day read this book and know that without his insatiable optimism and fierce loyalty, none of this could have occurred.

CONTENTS

Preface

A Letter to My Heart: A Story of Love Running Out of Time

Dear Heart,   *December 23, 2015*

We have been together for more than half a century. You knew me so well. I did not realize that I hardly knew you at all. That is, until one day in November 2015, when you were suddenly stricken. I struggled to get to the hospital. If I had needed to take five more steps to reach the doctor's office, I would have failed. But we got there just in time. You were in the final stage of a massive failure.

We somehow survived one week in the Cardiac Intensive Care Unit (CICU). Several times I heard you murmuring to me, "I don't think I can do it anymore." But you did, like you always have. One week later, a diagnosis came: Non-Compaction of Ventricular Myocardium (NVM)—an incurable heart condition with which I was born. I was told that symptoms are usually noticed very early in life, as a defective heart certainly gets in the way of normal living. The doctors had never seen a case with no symptoms before age fifty-two.

But you were smart. NVM is a diagnosis that was only established in 2006. Had you shown any symptoms earlier, it would only have been misdiagnosed and any treatment would have likely been either ineffective or counterproductive. So you labored on as if you were a normal heart. You helped me through my childhood when a boy had to be a man. You supplied my brain with oxygen so I could be accepted at Peking University at age fifteen and attend university in the U.S. at sixteen. We also took on impossible tasks, from the outbreak of SARS, the Sichuan Earthquake, and the Asiana Airlines crash, to the loss of Malaysia Airlines Flight 370 (MH370).

You were there through all the love and loss, rapture and agony, adventure and discovery, victory and defeat. You allowed me to experience the adventures of twenty lifetimes because you understood my goals.

Then, one day, after fifty-two years, you simply couldn't do it anymore. You had to stop. Allow me to be the first person to feel and express gratitude upon hearing "advanced stage heart condition" and "incurable disease" since every moment I have now seems like a wonderful gift. I am the luckiest person on earth because of you. You are the size of a giant grapefruit when you should be an orange. I know now how much you needed a rest. How selfish was I to be oblivious of your devotion? How pathetic would I be if I had the audacity to ask you to continue?

But I have a thought. You gave me fifty-two years of total devotion. I am asking you to give me an opportunity to reciprocate. You have been adjusting yourself to compensate for my desired pace. It is time for me to be sensitive to any subtle signals from you in the future, and adjust my pace according to your needs, because I know you and I both have unfinished business.

It was you who drove me to help people. We made a pact that our lives would be about the deliverance of people from suffering and making the world a better place.

We have done so much for the Employee Assistance Program (EAP) around the world, especially in bringing it to China. Wouldn't you like to see it help millions more people, making both the workplace and home full of love and empathy?

Together, we went to hundreds of cities, helping parents learn how to raise their children. Wouldn't you like to see these hundreds of thousands of those kids become great parents themselves? I would love share my path with others who seek a life with meaning. I want to inspire them and pass on the gift of giving; that would be a wonderful gift to the world.

Be it a day or another few decades, let's continue this partnership in service to family, to humanity, and ultimately, to God. Wherever and whenever this journey eventually ends, it will have been a life with meaning.

We are about to start our fifty-third year together. For me, it's more like Year One. I feel like a newborn baby. I am looking forward to this brand new journey.

Love, Paul Yin

Chapter 1

INHALE

The sun shines today also.
~Ralph Waldo Emerson, *Nature*

MH370

It was as if the very heavens had inhaled the entire jumbo jet. On March 8, 2014, Malaysia Airlines Flight 370 lost radar contact while en route from Kuala Lumpur, Malaysia, to Beijing, China. Two hundred and thirty-nine people were on board. No one knew if it had crashed, or been hijacked, or had undergone something else entirely.

The family members and friends of those passengers were waiting at the Beijing airport for their loved ones to arrive. The Arrival Boards shouted *delay!* at those waiting. And later, instead of greeting their friends and family after what was supposed to be a routine flight, they were given instructions to gather at the Lido Hotel near the airport to receive any updates on the plane's whereabouts.

The Lido Hotel was only a ten-minute drive from my home. As soon as I heard the news, I headed straight there.

The hotel lobby was crammed to capacity with families of MH370 passengers. I slowly walked through the crowd. The heavy weight of their despair settled squarely on my shoulders. I noticed an elderly lady sitting on the floor who was crying. I sat down beside her while tears began rolling in single streams down my cheeks. I held her hands, and I closed my eyes; she put her head on my shoulder and started crying louder. I wrapped my arms around her to comfort her. She cried and cried and her shoulders shook.

I moved to the next person, and I held that person's hands. My own tears flowed freely. In a sea of strangers, having someone caring to be with them at their darkest moment was what these people needed. I also knew that I was going to need more help. A lot of it.

The disappearance of MH370 was unprecedented. No one was prepared or trained to handle an event of this magnitude. But it felt like every single moment I had experienced in my life thus far had prepared me for this exact moment in time. Gwen; Dr. Frank; Paul-the-ticket-man; Rudy; the visa officer; my professors; and especially the events of Asiana 214; every connection with every person I ever met was a connection I had needed to make. It all started when I took a daring leap of faith in search of a life that had meaning.

Chapter 2

LOOK! I'M STILL FLYING!

*I learned this, at least, by my experiment: that if one advances
confidently in the direction of his dreams, and endeavors to live
the life which he has imagined, he will meet with a success
unexpected in common hours.*
~ Henry David Thoreau, *Walden*

Newsletter: December 31, 1980 (age sixteen)

Dear friends,

I am writing this letter a few days before New Year's Eve in America. I figured a newsletter would be a good way to stay in touch with all of you.

Many of you have asked me why I made this decision to leave China and come to California. At just fifteen years of age I was accepted into the most prestigious university in China. My friends and family viewed me as an anomaly and thought that this was the start of inevitable success for me. However, after one year at the university, I looked with disdain down the long, straight, mundane highway of my potentially successful life. I would have a successful career. I would marry. I would have an ideal life. But I yearned for more. I wanted a life that would have meaning. So, I packed my bags and left Peking University. With my parents' blessing, I got on a plane to pursue studies in the U.S.

It's true that I was always regarded as the good little boy who never caused any trouble. But few people knew that starting around the second grade, I wrote all the sick notes for my classmates who wanted to skip school because I could mimic their parents' handwriting. I also did homework for friends in exchange for cigarettes and helped them cheat at exams for beer. I was the boy who on a holiday broke every window at school with a slingshot. I was also the one who aimed and shot fireworks through the third-floor window of a neighborhood apartment building and started a piece of furniture on fire. I was an expert at not getting caught.

I didn't do all these things because I was a bad boy; I did them because I was terribly bored. School was easy and exams were a piece of cake. I entered the best university in China only eight years after I started first grade. And, as one of the youngest students at Beijing University, I was set to graduate in four years' time. My parents were proud of me. Others envied me. But being on a well-paved golden path seemed to me to be the worst possible life! It may be what everyone else wanted. But not me!

When I imagined this life that seemed expected of me, I heard the faint flutter of an eagle's wings calling me elsewhere. An eagle does not belong in a cage! I wanted the freedom to explore, expand, contemplate, take chances, make mistakes, and even fail. I wanted to know what a bird's-eye-view really looked like. Instead of the well-paved golden path of someone else's design, I wanted to find my own path. If I did crash, I'd be smiling as I hit the ground, safe in the knowledge that I once had soared.

When I arrived here in California to begin my studies, I landed in Los Angeles with ninety-seven dollars in my pocket, which was essentially my family's life savings. Two days later, I started washing dishes at a restaurant to earn my tuition money. After each twelve-hour workday, my hands and back would be aching.

> If I did crash, I'd be smiling as I hit the ground, safe in the knowledge that I once had soared.

A month later, I started my present job at a motel on Colorado Boulevard cleaning rooms and doing just about everything else that needed to be done. There were three small storage rooms. I asked the boss if I could squeeze all of the items into two of the storage rooms and live in the third rent free. He allowed me to do that and now I have my own room: seven feet by seven feet of grand spaciousness. I somehow fit a bed, a desk, a refrigerator, and a small cabinet into it. During the day, I put all my things on the bed. At night, I dump them on the floor so I can sleep. Because of the lack of ventilation, on a hot day it can be over one hundred degrees in the room, even at midnight. I also have to wait until someone checks out of their room to use the toilet!

But, I love every minute of it because this small room is my world! This is not a cage. It is a perch, a runway, and my first piece of sky. I have no place to cook, and I can't afford to eat out (although I did go to a fast-food place called McDonald's once). So, I buy vegetables that I can eat raw and, of course, bread. Day-old bread is half price. A gallon of milk is not very expensive either. I think I have drunk less than a gallon of milk since I was weaned fifteen years ago. Here I can drink it all the time. I am in heaven!

Public transportation in Los Angeles isn't that convenient, so I'm unable to get around much. I take the bus to and from school. That's more than two hours of travel time!

It does get scary at night. One night I was stopped by two young boys, possibly younger than I, but definitely bigger than I. Scared and not knowing what to do, I instinctively got into a martial arts pose. One of the boys yelled, "Bruce Lee!" and they both ran away. I had no idea who Bruce Lee was, but I suspected he was good at martial arts. On that day I decided that my American name is Bruce.

If you must know, I really have no idea when or if I'll ever return to China. I will grow and change, and so will China. Any promises I make now would be irresponsible. I miss you all, and I would love to receive letters from you. I may not be able to write back every time because, frankly, postage can be a major burden for me financially. I can, however, make a promise to you: once a year, a newsletter will arrive at your place. When you see it, you can say to yourself: "So the boy hasn't crashed yet!" Ha!

Love, Bruce

Learning the Gift of Giving

I welcomed that first New Year all by myself in America. As much as I put on a brave face, it was probably the loneliest I had ever felt in my life even though I had experienced severe loneliness before.

In 1966, when I was three, the Cultural Revolution began in China. During this chaotic period, it seemed as though the whole country was turned upside down. School students locked up their teachers in classrooms and on campuses across the country.

My parents, both teachers, were often forced to remain with their students for days, weeks, even months at a time, without being able to come home. It broke their hearts to leave their young child home alone, but unfortunately, they had no choice at the time. While I was home by myself, I learned to cook and sew before I could even write.

When I was four, my father thought I should have more adult supervision than what I was receiving. He put me on a train alone, with fifty cents in my pocket, to travel the four hundred and ten miles from Beijing to my grandma's place in Qingdao. It was the only place, in those hard days, where an adult could be at home all the time. I finally found my grandma after the twenty-hour train ride. I had become a seasoned solo traveler and a survivalist at four years of age.

By the time I was seven years old and my sister, Sherry, was two, I was considered old enough to be the full-time caregiver for her back at our home. I took on so much responsibility that sometimes I felt almost like I was her father. I cooked, fixed her hair, and taught her girls' games so she could play with others. When she outgrew one of her dresses, I, having only a basic knowledge of sewing, took the entire dress apart, traced all the pieces one inch larger on a bedsheet, and sewed the bedsheet together to make a larger sized dress.

One day, attempting to cook, I chopped off the tip of my right index finger. Bleeding profusely and in severe pain, I ran around the neighborhood looking for help. Finding none, I walked home, pulled some cotton from the quilt, and stuck it on my fingertip. Then, I got back to cooking and made up plates for both of us.

I didn't feel lonely then because I trusted that mommy might show up at the door at any moment. That moment could be anytime—maybe even three weeks away, but I still had complete confidence in her return.

However, now that I was in California and I had chosen this path for myself, I knew I would be alone for several years to come. The excitement of living in the New World was quickly wearing off, and at times I felt very lonely.

I did have several relatives in Los Angeles as well as some Chinese friends. They were all wonderful people. However, almost every Chinese person I met saw me as this "poor little thing who just escaped the claws of communism." Their kindness almost always came across as condescending. They'd talk about the evils of communism, such as "sharing wives," which wasn't even true. When I tried to correct them, they'd insist that I had been brainwashed and needed reeducation. "You need to study hard. We can tell that you don't study because you don't even wear glasses. All good students wear glasses," I was told. "Why are you reading poetry and philosophy? You should study accounting or computer science. These are practical. You are a brainwashed idealist, a victim of communist education!" To my Chinese family and friends in LA, I felt that I was always wrong and had no right to speak my mind.

> *You should study accounting or computer science. These are practical.*

I came to America for my freedom, but somehow I walked right into a culture where everyone around me tried to hijack my life from me. I began to hate this environment. Consequently, I decided to avoid them as much as possible.

I was told that my college had a program where people from the community sign up to be one-on-one friends with international students. One woman had specifically asked for a student from China. Being the only one from China, I jumped at the opportunity.

A week later, a woman named Gwen Singh picked me up at school and took me to her home for dinner. She was a Caucasian lady around seventy years old. She wore a pink dress with matching pink pearls, and she carried a big purse. Her hair was curled around her head in fat white rolls. She looked like a kind elderly grandma. Before I could even introduce myself, she reached into her purse and offered me a thick pink Canada mint.

I was curious about why she had an Indian surname. When I raised that exact question over tea that evening, she told me about an event in India in the 1920s called the Civil Disobedience Movement. She then motioned to an old oak credenza in the dining room. She blew a light cloud of dust off the handle of the top drawer, which shimmered like pixie dust in the bright rays of the setting sun. Inside the drawer was a manila folder which housed her beloved poetry from the young Sikh revolutionary who stole her heart.

She explained to me that he was a comrade of Gandhi in the 1940s. While this woman was in college, those warriors who struggled alongside Gandhi were glorified in the media, and like any intellectual, culture-savvy girl at the time, she was swept off her feet by such a highly regarded young man.

She looked over my head off in the distance as she told me that they rushed into marriage after falling swiftly in love, and that they never were blessed with children. After his death, Gwen went on to become a school principal for the rest of her widowed life. She retained an interest in the affairs of Asia, which was why she enjoyed befriending me as a wide-eyed *protégé*.

Although we met only once or twice a month, Gwen became my American mother. Through her, I got a pass into American culture and met many new friends. There were baseball games, museums, community events, concerts, the church, and volunteerism.

My first visit to a church took some arm-twisting. Gwen had asked me a few times if I'd like to go to church with her. I had always been curious about the church, but I was reluctant to go. It wasn't because I was "brainwashed" in China. Instead, it was because I had come here to free myself from outside forces trying to control my life. I saw the church, with its Bible and ministers, as just a different version of an organization that tells people what to do and how to behave. I was not looking to walk from one form of indoctrination into another, however different that may be. However, Gwen assured me that the church she went to not only tolerated differences but encouraged them. There would also be no pressure about joining the church. I'd only be a visitor. Eventually, I decided to give it a try.

It was a late September Sunday when I entered a church for the first time. I was struck by the friendliness of the people. I sat through the service, standing up, sitting down, opening the Bible as others did, and moving my lips in silence when they all sang. I was mesmerized by the beauty of the music from the choir.

The pastor was a soft-spoken man and short in stature. He talked about the book of Philippians in the Bible and the apostle Paul. The pastor explained that Paul was a man who vowed not to act in a self-serving manner. As I sat on the hard pew, I flipped through the Bible Gwen had placed into my hands before we got in the car. I read Philippians for myself. *Put others above myself?* I was intrigued by the apostle Paul.

Near the end of the service, people lined up to walk to the front. I followed. As I got close, I saw that people were putting money into a box. I ducked my head down and shoved my hands into my empty pockets, but Gwen gently nudged me and dropped a folded up ten dollar bill in my hand.

For our next outing, Gwen took me to the Los Angeles Philharmonic concert. It was sublime! Music was a big part of my life. From age six, I had performed regularly on stage, from conducting, to singing, from dancing, to theater. I once conducted a ten thousand-member chorus! Immediately, the Dorothy Chandler Pavilion lodged a permanent magnet on my soul. I was drawn to return countless times to immerse myself in the life-giving breath of the music.

I recalled a little detail from my visit with Gwen, which was a sign at the ticket office. It said: "Student Rush Tickets $5: One Hour Before the Concert!" The following week I took the bus to the Dorothy Chandler Pavilion and waited for seven o'clock to arrive so I could purchase my Student Rush Ticket. But when it was seven, I hesitated.

Frankly, I had to count every penny. Five dollars may not seem like a lot, but that was a quarter of my food budget for the week. Just as I was standing there undecided, a gentleman in a business suit came up to me and asked, "Young man, are you looking to get a ticket to the concert?"

"Yes, sir."

"Okay. My name is Paul. I happen to have a spare ticket this evening. Would you like to have it?"

"Really?" I couldn't believe what I was hearing.

"I have season tickets. I have two tickets for every series. Usually I take a client to the concert. But occasionally, when I do not have a client with me, I have an extra ticket. I always give my free ticket to a young student who loves music, just like you, under one condition."

"What condition?" I was curious.

"You have to promise me that one day when you become financially independent, when you have the resources, you must give a ticket to a student just like yourself. One day will you pass on the gift of giving?"

"Yes, I promise!"

"Young man, you are not from here, are you?"

"No, sir. I am from China."

"Oh, China! In that case, I'd like you to pass on the gift of giving to China, your homeland. Would you do that?"

> I might not change the world, but I'll be sure to pass on the gift of giving!

I didn't hesitate. "Yes, I will. I promise!"

He handed me his ticket. It was front row center, the best seat.

"Thank you!"

"No, thank *you!* Your promise, if kept, is worth so much more than this ticket. I only gave you a ticket. But you may change the world."

"I might not change the world, but I'll be sure to pass on the gift of giving!" I really wasn't sure how I would do that, but I never forgot this promise.

I started coming to the Dorothy Chandler Pavilion every week by myself. Incredibly, most of the time, all I needed to do was stand there and someone would give me a ticket.

One day, as I sat inside listening to Schubert's *Unfinished Symphony*, I thought about the huge debt I was building up. I would have a lot of giving to do one day. I was also reminded of how the minister at church had taught about the apostle Paul. Now, I had met another Paul. I was beginning to like this name. On my way home that evening, I decided to change my English name to Paul.

Give Your Dream a Chance

During my first three years of college in California, I took several psychology courses. I had become curious about the field since it wasn't offered in Chinese universities.

Originally, I found it very confusing. Every professor had a different view of psychology. It seemed they all belonged to a different school of thought! There was the "behind every twisted behavior is a twisted molecule" type, the "beyond freedom and dignity" deterministic behaviorists, and the "blame it on your mother" psychoanalysts, and so on. While taking the developmental psychology class, I kept saying to myself, "I don't remember any of these phases while I was growing up in China!" I was about to give up.

Then, I met Dr. Zimmermann. She was professional, friendly, and had a great sense of humor. Instead of saying, "you will agree with me if you want a decent grade," Dr. Zimmermann would ask me, "Paul, what was your experience?" She would reply, "Oh, that is so very interesting!" She encouraged me to think independently and to discuss my thoughts with her. Instead of the authoritarian holder of truth, she was the listener, collaborator, and facilitator.

After her class, and just before I left for my first summer vacation back in China, I changed my major to psychology. I didn't do so because I wanted to be a psychologist. In fact, I was quite sure that I would never want to become a psychologist. But I wanted to understand people. I was convinced that whatever profession I eventually chose or ended up in, knowledge of psychology and understanding of people would be useful.

As planned, I returned to China for my summer vacation. Since I was the only person around who had studied in the U.S., everyone I knew wanted to talk to me and know what it was like. I had already published some of my poetry which gave me a little "celebrity status," at least in my circles. Somehow, everyone really thought I was going to be a great something or other. Was I going to be a mad scientist? A Hollywood actor? An economist? How about a lawyer? Banker? Composer? Conductor? When I told people that my major was psychology, everyone became even more intrigued. It was something that none of them had ever thought about.

"So, you will be treating crazy people when you graduate?" they'd ask.

"No, psychology is not about crazy people. Most of the time we benefit normal people who may need help," I explained.

"Oh, now I understand. You mean, it's like *political thought correction?*" Political thought correction was what China currently had to offer for those with mental health issues. Suddenly people began to imagine that I would be like the very people I tried all my life to elude.

"Can you read my mind? Do you know what I am thinking at this moment?"

"Can you put me to sleep and get me to do things against my will?"

"You can control people's minds! Wow! You can be the next Chairman Mao, only a scientific one!"

Hardly anyone really gave me a chance to explain what psychology was. They simply wanted me to confirm their preconceived notions. Suddenly, I turned from the Prodigal Son into the Exotic Beast—Circus Freak. To my surprise, the only person who gave me a chance to explain, and who actually listened, was Rudy.

Rudy had come into my life in a strange way. In the spring of 1978, when I was only fourteen, someone knocked on our door at 6:30 in the morning. We opened the door. Outside stood a young man we had never met.

"Is this where Mr. Yin lives?" He asked this with a wide smile chiseled above his square chin. He wore thick black-rimmed glasses and a shock of his hair was sticking out horizontally from the left side of his head. His gray button-down shirt had never met an iron.

"That would be me," replied my father.

"Mr. Yin, you don't know me. But I am a former student of Mr. Fu in Jinan, whom you have met at least twice." Jinan was a town about two hundred and fifty miles away.

"Yes, I do remember him," my father said.

"Mr. Fu told me that you were the most wonderful human being he had ever met, and that you live in Beijing. I have a dream. I always wanted to be a composer. This year, the Academy of Music finally resumed operation after eleven years. The entrance exam is this month here in Beijing. Frankly, I have never had formal music lessons, but I have a passion. Everyone tells me that only the best of the best from the past eleven years possibly stand a chance. I am just a carpenter. But I will regret it for the rest of my life if I do not at least give it a try. I have no money to stay in hotels. I have spent all my savings on the train ticket to get here. Do you think I could live with your family for a while?" His smile remained right there on his face. Did he ever stop smiling?

> *"I wonder if I could live with your family for a while?" His smile remained right there on his face. Did he ever stop smiling?*

What an audacious request coming from a complete stranger, I thought. But my father's reply surprised me.

"What is your name, son?"

"Rudy Qingchuan."

"I like a young man with a dream," said my father. "Every dream should be given a chance. You are welcome to live with my family while you prepare for the exam."

My mom looked wide-eyed at my dad, but she stepped aside so Rudy could enter.

For about three weeks, Rudy lived in our small two-room apartment. I watched him study and compose. He almost perfected "Twinkle, Twinkle, Little Star." *He'll finish last,* I thought. But he worked hard. Every day, he'd take a long walk outside. Each time, he'd come back with a discarded piece of wood he'd picked up. "We don't need firewood," I told him. He just smiled that same wide smile and blinked at me from behind his thick glasses.

After he finished the exams, he asked my father. "Is there a place where you can borrow some tools for me? I still have a couple of weeks to wait for the results. I have some carpentry skills that I picked up, and I would like to repay you by making some furniture with the wood I picked up."

Two weeks later, Rudy got the results. He probably came close to finishing last. But he had given his dream a chance.

We sat at the table Rudy had just finished making, having a beer to send him off. My dad told him, "I am glad you gave your dream a chance. Don't be discouraged. You will have bigger and better dreams. If you keep at it, one of them will come true."

Over the years that followed, Rudy had many new dreams. He attempted multiple ventures. None of them succeeded.

But now, the day before I left to go back to the U.S., he knocked on our door again at 6:30 in the morning. He spent the day with me. I told him about psychology, and he listened attentively.

As I continued, Rudy's face began to light up. His eyes grew wide behind his glasses. "Paul! What you are studying is something really different, and I think it is something that China will need. Consider me your assistant, your agent, your promoter, your dedicated servant on this venture for life!" Rudy stood up and started pacing. "We will need to go big! We should probably start to practice giving speeches. How are you at public speaking?" He jerked his head in my direction and sized me up.

I shrugged my shoulders.

"Maybe there are other things we can work on first," he conceded.

Rudy was so far ahead of me on this. I had not thought that far yet. I was not even committed to psychology. But Rudy was a dreamer. He always dreamt big dreams. He hugged me tightly. "One of us will eventually have a dream come true. Yours is as good as mine!" he said.

Making the World a Better Place, One Smile at a Time

When I was nineteen and still in college in California with an undecided career path, Gwen introduced me to her dentist, Dr. Bill Frank. A man with broad shoulders and an even broader smile, Dr. Frank's love for humanity was most extraordinary.

His wife Ruth was a polio survivor. She had given a speech at the United Nations which launched a remarkable program called Polio Plus. Working with the United Nations, Rotary International would raise over two hundred million dollars to eradicate polio and nine other diseases from the face of the earth by giving immunizations to all children in every nation. (That number would eventually end up at over 1.2 billion.) As district governor, and one of the people most responsible for launching the program in the first place, Dr. Frank would be dedicating much of his time and energy to this effort.

> *If you can commit yourself to this cause, you'd be doing it for no other reason than to help complete strangers.*

One day, as I squinted into the bright light over the dental chair, he asked me, "Do you know someone with polio, Paul?"

He held one of my cheeks open with his mouth mirror and poked at my teeth with his dental pick. I replied, "O-oo, not pershonally. but I haf sheen peop-o wif po-yee-yo."

Dr. Frank paused and pulled the mouth mirror out. "You know what … how would you like to be my volunteer assistant?"

I was delighted! "Of course, I would like to do that!"

"But you need to understand how important this is for you. Let me tell you why. We are saving millions of children, but I am doing this partly because of Ruth. She's a polio survivor. I don't want to see other children suffer like she did. As much as it is a noble thing to do, there is still a little bit of personal, selfish desire behind it. For you, it's different. You don't know anyone with polio. If you can commit yourself to this cause, you'd be doing it for no other reason than to help complete strangers.

"The purest and greatest form of *true love* for humanity is a love for complete strangers. Once you learn to leave self-interest behind and love humanity as a whole, then you become the greatest beneficiary."

Before I left, he hugged me tightly. "We will be great partners!"

Dr. Frank reminded me of my dad. My dad was one of the most benevolent people I knew.

One day back in 1973, when I was ten, my father came home with an old peasant and a dirty young boy. The boy pooped on our bed almost as soon as he got into the house. It was a mess.

My father had been riding home on his bike from his job as a local school teacher when he saw the old peasant wandering aimlessly on the street with the boy. He stopped to ask if he could help them. They were from a village almost one hundred miles away.

The boy had been diagnosed with an incurable disease, but the old man couldn't remember the name of it. They were told that only hospitals in Beijing would be able to treat him. His only chance would be to take him to there. So, the peasant put the boy on his bike and rode all the way to Beijing. It was the first time that they had ever left their home county. Once he arrived in the city, he had no idea what to do. He had no money, spoke a dialect that only a few understood, and was completely illiterate. He had been wandering around for two days.

"Come home with me. We will help you!"

Just like that, we had two complete strangers living in our home for three weeks. My parents took them to the best hospital in Beijing. They paid all the medical bills with money we didn't have. Dad had to take a loan from the teacher's labor union to make ends meet. But we spared no effort.

Three weeks later, they left.

In 1975, about two years later, I heard someone shouting from the street. "Mr. Yin? Does Mr. Yin live here?" I looked outside. It was that old peasant. Unfortunately, the man's son did not survive, but he wanted to thank us for our benevolence. He told us that they had just had a bountiful harvest. He had packed up more than sixty pounds of grain, fruits, and vegetables from the harvest and rode his bicycle all the way to Beijing.

> *I didn't remember your address and I can't read, so I have been shouting from block to block for the past two days. Beijing is so big!*

"I didn't remember your address and I can't read, so I have been shouting from block to block for the past two days. Beijing is so big!" Indeed, the population of Beijing at that time was around eight million.

My parents had been showing me by example that we need to love our fellow men, strangers included. In a way, Dr. Frank was just like my father. And Dr. Frank was right. I was the primary beneficiary.

After a Polio Plus event in early 1986, Dr. Frank and I had dinner together. He asked me, "Paul, have you decided on psychology as your future profession?"

"No, I'm really not sure."

He chuckled. "I guess you aren't someone who will settle on doing one thing. You might host the Chinese version of *The Tonight Show*. You might be the greatest Chinese poet since Li Tai Po. Or, perhaps you will become the music director of the Chinese Philharmonics. You could also be a quantum physicist or a famous philosopher. Maybe you will be the Chinese ambassador to the United Nations. On the side, you just may be the Chinese Sigmund Freud as well."

I thought seriously for a while and finally gave my response.

"To be perfectly honest, I still have no idea what I want to do in the future. I am not finished exploring. But I want to thank you for helping me find a direction. I now know with absolute certainty that, whatever I do in the future, I want it to enable me to say at the end of my life, 'This world is now a better place because I was here.' I want to live a life that resembles the examples set before me by my father, and by you. I, too, want to leave a legacy in my wake where humanity has been forever changed by the footprints I have left behind."

"Psychology Has No Place in Chinese Society, and You Know It!"

When I first decided to study in the United States, my plan was to go back to China every three years. But traveling that far was expensive, and tuition took a large portion of my money. It took a lot of overtime work to save enough money to make the trip possible. However, in 1986, when I was twenty-two years old, I was able to return to China and spend six weeks at home.

Everything went as planned until the day I went to get my visa to return to California. Since I was enrolled in college, maintained a full-time status, and had yet to graduate, this should have been a mere formality. However, it turned out to be an extraordinary event that changed the direction of my life.

I went to the U.S. Embassy just a few days before my scheduled flight back to LA. I casually approached the visa officer's desk and handed him my papers. After perusing my papers, the visa officer frowned.

> *I am sorry to tell you that your visa is denied.*

"Mr. Yin, I see that you are a psychology major." His eyes narrowed slightly as he looked over the top of the papers at me.

"Yes, sir," I replied. "A bit unusual for a Chinese person?"

"I'd say." He smooshed his lips together tightly with a slight shake of his head and sniffled sharply. "Mr. Yin, I am sorry to tell you that your visa is denied."

He shoved the paperwork back in my direction. "Mr. Yin, your choice of major is a clear indication that you plan to stay in the U.S. after you graduate and have no plan whatsoever to return to China."

"What?" I pushed the papers back toward him. "There's nothing here that would imply that! How can you make that judgment just from my choice of a major? Please reconsider!"

"Well, let's not kid ourselves." He looked at me with a patronizing smile and leaned in close to my face. Very slowly, enunciating each word as if he were speaking to a little child, he said, *"Psychology has no place in Chinese society and you know it."*

"How can you say that? China is changing fast, and psychology will be extremely important and very much in demand one day."

"I'm sure it will be," he said. "But not anytime soon." He picked up his pen and looked around on his desk in an effort to busy himself with some other task to imply that I was dismissed.

I was angry. But I knew about the supreme power of the visa officer. It was time to be tactful rather than emotional. "Please give me an opportunity to prove otherwise."

"What? And change your major?" he scoffed. "Nah, it's too late for that!"

I had never really been described as stubborn, but something about this officer's attitude and the unexpected denial of what should have been a routine thing made me want to dig my heels in. "No. I chose psychology and I am committed to it," I heard myself say. "So, what can I do to convince you that I will be coming back and that psychology *does* have a place in Chinese society?"

He sighed. He crossed his arms and looked thoughtfully up at the ceiling. Then he raised his eyebrows again and said, "You may reapply for your visa in thirty days. In the meantime, if you can secure a job offer that will be guaranteed upon completion of your degree—and I mean a master's degree as a bachelor's in psychology is worthless—then I may reconsider."

"See you in thirty days then!" I collected my paperwork and turned away from the visa officer.

When I left the embassy, I was beside myself. It was clear that he had given me an impossible task. How could anyone give a job offer to an undergraduate student for a job several years in the future? It made no sense and I wasn't even sure if that would be legal. But I had at least secured a thin lifeline. I was not about to abandon my course.

I started job searching. I did have to admit, the visa officer had a point. Other than the medical psychiatry department in a few hospitals, there were no jobs in China in psychology. Psychology had vanished from the Chinese universities for many years. Just two years prior, a few select universities had resumed offering psychology courses, but the professors were mostly medical doctors.

To most people, even in the universities, psychology was for the worst-case schizophrenics. What was called "counseling" in the west was called "political thought correction" and was done by "political officers." I thought maybe I could get a job teaching psychology at a university. So, I went to talk to a university that had just established a psychology department. They almost laughed right in my face. "When was the last time an undergraduate applied for a future job as a professor?" they had mused.

I left the university dejected. I had a feeling that they'd be laughing at my audacity and sharing this story with friends and colleagues for years to come.

When I had initially settled on psychology as my major, I wasn't totally committed to it. But now I apparently was, thanks to the visa officer. The more I thought about it, though, the more I began to see psychology in China as a mission. It would take someone who knew the culture and understood psychology. I was convinced there *was* a place for psychology in China. I was also convinced that I was the person who could establish that.

But if I couldn't find a job? I kept plugging away. Eventually, I did find a university that was "considering starting a psychology department in the future." After some serious convincing and arm-twisting, they gave me a job offer letter. I think we both understood that the letter was not legally binding in any shape or form. But for my purpose, it was just fine. I took the letter to the U.S. Embassy.

The visa officer was surprised. He reviewed my paperwork while his lower lip stuck out and his head bobbed up and down. "Impressive," he said. "I like your commitment. I do hope that you will come back and open up the Chinese market for psychology. It will not be easy. But it will indeed be a good thing."

I had been angry at this man a mere thirty days ago. Now I was thankful for this draconian visa officer who happened to take my case. Maybe it was just an accident. But secretly I was hoping that it was not. Maybe God had sent him to help me recognize that I was part of His divine plan.

Wait, did I actually say the G word?

CHAPTER 3

BROKEN COMPASS

Even with these dark eyes, a gift of the dark night,
I go to seek the shining light.
~Gu Cheng, "A Generation"

Life with No Regrets

I returned to California committed to studying psychology. Although I became a much more focused student, I still found time to venture into other things.

I drove a friend to her cello master class at the University of Southern California. During the morning break, the master, Dr. Eleanor Schoenfeld, saw me standing outside. "It's windy and cold today. Why don't you sit inside?" Then, during class, she asked a question. The class fell silent. But she saw a murky smile cross my face and asked me, "Do you have something to share with us?" I shared my thoughts and she was delighted. Afterwards, she asked, "Can you come to every class? I enjoy having your input." So, although I didn't play the cello at all, I sat through a year of cello master classes. This is also where I met Mehli Mehta, the father of Zubin Mehta; Lynn Harrell; and a host of other great musicians.

One day, I saw in the papers that the second Los Angeles Marathon would take place on March 1, 1987. I decided to give it a try. I knew many people had run marathons. But for me, this represented the impossible. When I was seven, I started having problems with my knees. Often while walking, my knees would suddenly buckle and I would collapse. Mom took me to all the best hospitals in Beijing. The doctors told us that it was untreatable. An operation might correct the problem, but there was a greater than fifty-fifty chance that it might also make it worse. The conclusion was that I may not be able to walk when I got to a certain weight, probably by the time I became a teenager.

But now, I wanted to show myself that I could do anything. I wanted to show myself that I could do anything. So, I signed up. There were more than 15,000 people at the marathon. After the starting gun sounded, it took half an hour before I even got to the starting gate. I started to run. A few hours later, as I was within a mile of the finish line, my knees began to buckle and collapse. I began to move sideways and back and forth like a drunk. A Red Cross van followed me and monitored me closely. But since I was so close, I guess they decided to give me a chance to finish. I collapsed the moment I crossed the finish line.

I was taken toward the Red Cross tent, but it was full.

"I am fine now. Maybe you can just lean me against a tree," I told the technician.

I leaned against a tree and smiled. Here was a kid not supposed to be able to walk who just finished a marathon. I had just proven to myself that I could do anything if I decided to be totally committed to it. I felt like Superman!

My Mentors

But what Superman needed right now more than anything else was psychology classes. A few friends suggested that I should transfer to a university with a more prominent psychology department. But what kept me at California State University was that I thought I had some of the best psychology professors in the world there. Maybe other people wouldn't agree. But they were the perfect professors for me. They gave me exactly what I needed. It seemed as if they were specifically sent to earth just to teach me.

Dr. David Lawrence was by all accounts not the most popular professor. There was a good reason for that, and it all started on day one. Dr. Lawrence gave his opening speech.

"Let me tell you how my class works. If you have a problem with it, you have two weeks to drop the class. If you listen attentively in class, take perfect notes, do all your assignments perfectly and, on the exams, answer all the questions correctly according to what I have taught you, you will get a C."

Everyone gasped.

"There is only one way to get an A in my class. This class is not about passively absorbing. It is about active participation. Somewhere along the line, you need to exhibit your thinking by disagreeing with me in some way. But that can be dangerous. I do not require that you convince me that you are right and I am wrong. But I need to be able to see your line of logic and see your thinking process. If you disagree with me just for the sake of disagreeing, with no sensible reason, then you get an F! But if you can show good sense and good thinking behind it, you get an A!"

Most of the traditional "good students" were scared away. I stayed. I stayed because Dr. Lawrence was exactly the kind of professor I wanted. I didn't mind getting an occasional F. Grades meant nothing to me. I just wanted to learn. I wanted to understand. I wanted to think independently.

I became a fixture at Dr. Lawrence's office during his office hours. We talked about many things. "Paul, you don't get the best grades," he said, "but you are my favorite student. Do you know why? Because your only quest is seeking total understanding. Do you know when you'll know that you truly understand something?"

"When?" I almost laughed looking at the smirk on Dr. Lawrence's face.

"When you forget it. Someone who remembers every little detail, every 1, 2, 3, and A, B, C, can't possibly understand a thing. Understanding and knowing are not at that level. A truly great psychologist never says to himself, 'Okay, I will use this technique now.' He doesn't even remember what technique he used. He just knows because he understands. You can be like that."

But the greatest gift to me from Dr. Lawrence came at the end of his life. One day, as I was walking in the hallway, Dr. Lawrence walked by.

"Paul, I'm glad I ran into you! Come to my office."

In his office, Dr. Lawrence told me that he had resigned from the school because he had cancer.

"I'm sorry to hear that." I was shocked and saddened.

"Don't be. Cancer is part of life."

Then, Dr. Lawrence told me about his experiences with illness.

"You know, Paul, when you get struck down by a major illness, people always encourage you to fight it with courage. I don't. To me, fighting against something is not a very healthy mental state. Cancer is part of me now. Why should I fight it? My strategy is to live in peace with it on friendly terms. Then after we have lived peacefully and amicably together for a while, I will ask it in a very nice way to go away."

"So, this is what you will do now?"

"No, this time it is different. The doctors told me that my cancer is completely treatable, but they would have to take off part of my face. I thought living without a face would lack dignity. I made the decision to not treat it. I have made a list of things that I always wanted to do but never had the time. Starting tomorrow, I will start doing them for as long as I have time."

A year or so later, I got a letter from Dr. Lawrence. It was obviously written a while before but just mailed out recently:

Don't be sad. There is no reason to feel sad. I lived the way I chose to. I died the way I chose to. I lived a life with no regret. Do not buy a wreath and spend money on my funeral. Instead, donate to your favorite charity or, better yet, give time to your favorite charity. But if you can, I would really like a few of you to get together to celebrate the conclusion to a life with no regret.

Dr. Lawrence didn't just teach psychology. He taught me about life.

Dr. Herb Goldberg is another professor who had a profound influence on me. He taught me how to truly listen. He taught me to not only look through someone's protective veil, but to appreciate it as well. My most memorable episode happened in a class in which two students kept interrupting and challenging the "scientific correctness" of Dr. Goldberg's methods.

"I appreciate your loyalty to your school of thought," Dr. Goldberg said. "I have no doubt that in your minds you are correct. I wouldn't be surprised that many others in this class thought the same."

Then he paused.

"A counseling session is not a debate where a winner emerges. We are in a profession to help people. So, you are presented with a choice: Would you rather be right? Or would you rather be effective? Would you rather be right? Or would you rather be helpful? Would you rather be right? Or would you rather save lives?"

The two students fell silent.

The true elder statesman at the school was Dr. Diamond. He was in his eighties when he taught me. He carried a knobby wooden cane and perched tiny round spectacles on his nose. Some said he was eighty-eight. Some said he was mentored by Freud. If so, perhaps that makes me a student of a student of the great Sigmund Freud! You can't imagine a more appropriate professor for History of Psychology than someone who literally lived through most of that history. On the first day of class, Dr. Diamond gave us his rules in his soft, slow speaking voice.

"No one can take notes. Anyone taking notes will be kicked out of the class. Notes have no value. There is nothing specific that you must remember. What you need is to listen, participate, think, and understand, so that in the end you *know*." He paused.

Then, he handed out a reading list of fifty books, most of which were over five hundred pages.

"This is your reading list. No one can possibly read all these books in eleven weeks. I bet you can't do more than ten percent of them. But these are not for you to finish. It does not matter which book you read, or which part of which book you read. Read what you can and especially what grabs you."

"What about the exams? How will we be graded?" The questions came.

"I knew someone would ask that! You are not here to study for the exams. I have not decided what to do for the exams yet. But if you listen, participate, think, read, and learn, you will do just fine."

Just like Dr. Lawrence, Dr. Diamond left most students in a fog. But that was exactly what I liked! I listened attentively to every word coming out of Dr. Diamond's mouth. I do not remember a single word of it today. So now I truly understand what Dr. Lawrence meant when he said, "You will truly understand something when you forget."

> *Truly great teachers make their students better than their teachers.*

There was no midterm. On the day of the final, Dr. Diamond said, "The final is an essay question. There is no length requirement. You may write one single sentence. You may write one hundred pages. If you cannot finish in class, you may write it at home and give it to me on Monday. Here is the question, "How am I thinking differently now, after this class, as compared to before taking this class?"

There is an old Chinese piece of wisdom that has been passed down which basically says, "Truly great teachers make their students better than their teachers." If the teacher is an egocentric person who thinks that he holds the truth, then the best the students can do is to approach the teacher's greatness, but never surpass it.

None of these professors pretended to be the holder of ultimate truth. They facilitated learning, thinking, exploration, and growth. I may not have been in the most famous university for studying psychology, but I certainly had the best professors I could possibly ask for.

The Duty of Genius

After receiving my master's in psychology, I took an internship position at a mental health center in Chinatown, Los Angeles. I hoped to be able to focus on the many Chinese people who lived in that area. But the Chinese people did not come. Very few of them were seeking mental health help, even though it was free. Those who did come didn't always tell me the truth. They were not good cooperative clients at all. I became frustrated. I started talking to Chinese people of different ages and backgrounds to try to understand this further. It slowly started to make sense.

There are two major reasons why Chinese people shy away from psychological intervention. First of all, there's an old Chinese saying which cautions, "Never exhibit your family's dirty laundry to outsiders. Saving face is the most important thing." I have known Chinese fathers to prohibit their daughter from reporting a rape because they did not want the "shame" it would bring to the family. The only thing they want outsiders to see are their good sides—things worth exhibiting or even flaunting. All problems are supposed to be dealt with internally.

Another reason that Chinese people shy away from psychology is because of all those frightening labels and terms. *Pathology, schizophrenia, mental disorder,* and *phobia* are labels that frighten people. The Chinese translations of these words make them sound even worse.

In America, if there is problem identified as an "illness," it illuminates the situation and actually takes pressure off. Treatment can begin. For the Chinese, they don't want it to be labeled "an illness." So, I avoided using these terms. I came as a trusted friend. I used psychological techniques, but I never presented myself as a psychological counselor.

> *Faced with these cultural inhibitions, if I sat in my office waiting for patients to come, I would be very disappointed.*

Faced with these cultural inhibitions, if I sat in my office waiting for patients to come, I would be very disappointed. If I wanted to help people, they had to know me and trust me *before* they had problems. I would have to be inside at least the close friend's circle of trust ahead of time. My degree and certificates wouldn't do. On top of this, the word "psychology" carried with it a stigma that caused people to take a step back and keep a respectful distance.

I started an experiment. I used weekends, holidays, and other free time to frequent churches, schools, clubs, community organizations, chambers of commerce, and other local Chinese gatherings to get to know people—actually, mostly to get people to know me. After I had become friends and gained trust, I could begin to help them. I was soon being introduced as "a close friend who is very good at helping people solve problems." As a friend, or friend of a friend, I began to penetrate those thick walls. I began to receive cases. I was able to help people who otherwise would never seek help. I received no income from this work, but I saw it as a learning experience. I was happy.

Other things were also happening in my life. I entered into a committed relationship with Karen, a young woman who had just arrived in America from China. I tried to teach her English and was paying for her college tuition.

On September 13, 1993, Karen and I had the privilege of hosting Gu Cheng, in my mind the greatest living Chinese poet, in our home. He and his wife helped celebrate my thirtieth birthday. We had a wonderful time. We talked all night into the morning. At length we discussed poetry, history, philosophy, religion, art, and humanity.

It was the most intellectual conversation I had since my days with Dr. Lawrence. I thoroughly enjoyed our time together, and I enjoyed further discussion while I drove them to the airport so they could fly back to New Zealand where they lived.

Just a few weeks later, I received the news that Gu Cheng had killed his wife and committed suicide himself. I was shocked. I also blamed myself for not noticing any red flags. Looking back, I could see there were some clear signs that I had missed. Karen was also worried since I myself was a poet. "You are so much like him. You are both poets, idealists, impractical people . . ." she said. We both began to question my direction in life.

At the time, Karen was a political refugee from China. She was not going to be able to go back to China for quite a while. What she needed was a settled, stable environment in the U.S. In order to support the two of us, I needed to get a good, secure job with a consistent income. I felt an obligation to offer her that stability.

I was learning a lot from my counseling work, but progress was slow. And now, Gu Cheng had died after passing through my door. Was my dream of becoming a psychologist not practical? Should I abandon it? I began to waver. Maybe it was time to settle down as a family man and become a practical person.

I decided to take a job unrelated to the field of psychology, working for the State of California. This is what the Chinese would call an "iron rice bowl" job. The work was easy and the pay was decent. Karen and I had time for home-cooked meals, baseball games, concerts, outings, and lots of travel. This was a beautiful life that most people would have loved to live. I began to settle into this new, albeit boring, lifestyle.

On our travels, we took a trip to Boston where a good friend of mine named Fa Mo lived. Fa Mo had adopted the lifestyle of a bachelor in Boston. He wore a narrow beard and mustache along with the quintessential beret, scarf, and three-quarter-length pea coat which many Bostonians donned. Unlike most Chinese, Fa Mo did not choose an American name for himself. His American name came from combining his Chinese names "Fa" and "Mo." Fa Mo became known as Farmer.

During our visit, Farmer drove me to what had become one of his favorite places in Boston to relax and contemplate life: Walden Pond. We talked while we circled around Walden Pond. Our friendship was such that we could, with ease, dig into deep philosophical conversation, and with the same ease, we could laugh lightheartedly over the simplest things. We talked about the significance of Walden Pond and the writings of Henry David Thoreau. Farmer and I both appreciated the spirit of transcendentalism and Thoreau's choice to live without borders.

However, what Farmer really wanted to discuss were my reasons for foregoing my dream to establish the field of psychology in China. He listened politely while I tried to justify my current choice of a stable job where I could live a decent life and keep food on the table. After I enumerated all of my excuses, he did not reply. He reached into his backpack and pulled out a book.

> *Don't bother to read the book. All you need to do is read the title!*

"Paul, I have to say I'm really surprised at the road you are choosing to take. I brought a little something that I'm hoping will get you to think."

I looked. It was a biography of the great German philosopher Ludwig Wittgenstein. The book was titled *The Duty of Genius.*

"Thank you, Farmer. It's been a while since I read a good book."

"Don't even bother to open the book."

I could tell by the way he clenched his jaw that he was upset. "What? What do you mean?" I was puzzled.

"The content of the book is irrelevant. Don't bother to read the book. All you need to do is to read the title!"

I was the last person he'd expected to sell out to practical reality. Farmer knew that I was limiting myself.

Flying Solo

I was thirty and still living with the "iron rice bowl" job in 1994. Karen and I decided to get married. Well, maybe I should say I decided to get married. Karen was reluctant. The wedding was postponed for one reason or another for almost a year. The truth was, we were practically married and only the formality was missing. I flew my parents to California for the wedding. Finally, I became a married man living a normal married life.

In 1995, just as the dream of establishing psychology in China was beginning to fade from my mind, I received a letter from Rudy.

Rudy's letter very emphatically told me that China may now be ready for psychology! He thought he could organize mental health education lecture tours for me that would be free to the public.

China may now be ready for psychology!

"Mental health is a buzz word that is appearing more and more frequently. I think it's time for you to come back and become the trailblazer!" Rudy's letter resonated in my thoughts as I, of course, packed my bag to learn more about his plan. I vaguely wondered if Rudy was dreaming too much again, but I was intrigued nonetheless.

I flew to Beijing to meet with Rudy to formalize our plans. From his briefcase, he pulled out pages and pages of notebook paper where he had written down notes, phone numbers, and names of people he was going to contact. I squinted uneasily at some of the strange diagrams he had sketched out.

"What is—?" But he was already explaining that he had taken the initiative to secure the lecture halls, and he was just putting the finishing touches on the marketing procedure. All I needed to do was to show up and talk!

Rudy was fired up. He started pacing. "What exactly do you think you will talk about for your lecture?" he asked. Then, before I could answer, he said, "Never mind! I just know you will be great! This is so exciting isn't it?" He waved his pencil in sharp little increments as if he were conducting a marching band. "This is exactly what Chinese people need right now! You will be the first to give it to them!"

My first lecture, which Rudy had organized, was to start at two o'clock in the afternoon. It was one thirty. There was a very large group of people lingering in the public square in front of the theater. I walked into the theater. It was empty. Were those people outside all here for the purpose of attending the lecture? I wondered. I waited.

At two o'clock, one man walked in.

"Are you here for the lecture?" I asked.

"Yes, I am. But is there actually going to be a lecture? This place is empty," he said as he looked around.

"Was the crowd outside here for the lecture? Do you know?" I asked.

"I think they were, but no one walked in. I think everyone wanted to see if anyone else is coming in. No one wants to be seen coming to a mental health lecture unless everybody comes in. Otherwise, people will think you have a crazy person in your family," he said.

"What made you come in then?" I wondered.

"I'm not from here. No one knows me. Besides, I really want to listen to what you have to say. So, uh, will there still be a lecture if I'm the only one here?"

I smiled. "Absolutely! But not here. If it is just you and me, let's find a place that's more comfortable. I see that there is a teahouse across the street. Let's go there and talk over a pot of tea. My treat!"

We sat down over a steaming pot of green tea. Taking a sip, he said, "If this were about physical health, I think everyone would have come in. Everyone wants longevity. But mental health is an entirely different matter."

"Do you think physical health and mental health are entirely different matters?" I asked.

"Are they not?"

"Your body is like a pharmacy. It is making so many different types of chemicals and medicines all the time, including things like stomach acid, hormones…"

"Oh, a pharmacy! I like this analogy!" I could see that I had gotten his attention.

"This pharmacy works automatically and perfectly. You never have to tell your stomach to make a certain amount of stomach acid because you are about to eat a sandwich and a bowl of soup. It always does it automatically and correctly. However, if you are psychologically imbalanced, if you are under stress, anxiety, and other unwanted emotions, your pharmacy has to make other chemicals to deal with those things. For instance, it may produce things that raise your blood pressure and heart rate. If this is happening all the time, what do you think will happen?"

"High blood pressure and heart disease?"

"Exactly! And what do you think it does to all those automatic and otherwise almost always perfect operations? It messes them up as well. Your stomach may produce too much acid, or too little."

My lone student looked concerned. "My manager was just diagnosed with heart disease and an ulcer. He has been under a lot of stress for several years now. Maybe that is the cause?"

"That is entirely possible. Your pharmacy can also produce chemicals like painkillers, disease fighters, and cancer fighters. Good mental health keeps your little personal pharmacy in perfect order."

"So," he said, "I should do my best never to have bad emotions. I should try to be happy all the time."

"I am not sure you can. If some stranger walks by and for no reason at all slaps your face, you're surely going to get angry. Otherwise, I'd suspect you have a major problem! In that situation, being angry is normal. Most of our negative emotions are simply normal human reactions. They are there for a reason. If you have no negative emotions whatsoever, then you are either a saint or a mental patient."

He laughed. "I don't think I am either!"

"Exactly!" I continued. "Good mental health is not about becoming a saint. We want negative emotions to happen with less frequency, less intensity, and not last for a long time. We want to be able to manage them better. But our goal is not to get rid of them entirely. In fact, one of the worst things you can do is to suppress your negative emotions."

"Now you are talking about me! Ha!" He laughed.

Our talk lasted for almost three hours.

In the end, my solo student said, "If those people only knew how helpful this is, they'd regret missing it for the rest of their lives! I have learned how to be physically healthier through mental health. I have learned how to be a better husband and father. I have learned how to better communicate with my co-workers. I think you have just changed my life!"

> *One lecture won't change your life. Let this be the beginning.*

"One lecture won't change your life. Let this be the beginning. Find some books and do some learning on your own. I think you will find it rewarding."

"You bet I will!"

My first lecture of my grand project had ended. I was ecstatic! Even though it was just for one person, the experience gave me confidence. I now knew I had the right stuff. I knew it was something that people needed. I knew if they did come, they would be able to embrace my concepts.

Upon learning that my lecture turned out to be only me and one person at a teahouse, Rudy was dejected. His smile waned and his excitement cooled to a black ember. "I'm sorry. I don't see how we can continue. I misjudged the situation. I guess we should cancel the rest of the tour."

"You're right. We should cancel the tour, but don't feel bad. This is a good start. It's good practice for me. I learned a lot. I am ready. But China isn't. We can try again in the future."

I sat alone on the plane back to the U.S.. I had mixed feelings. This trip was both a success and a failure. What should I do next? Was I going back to my very Americanized family life? Was I going to try again next year? What would Karen think? What I didn't know was that my marriage of less than a year was about to collapse.

Chapter 4

FOLLOWING THE COMET

It's a funny thing about coming home. Looks the same, smells the same, feels the same. You'll realize what's changed is you.
~ F. Scott Fitzgerald, *The Curious Case of Benjamin Button*

Night Sky

Karen was gone. She had moved out of the apartment. She couldn't explain what happened. She just didn't want to be married anymore. I remembered that she had never wanted to get married in the first place. I felt guilty, betrayed, and sad.

I went three days without eating, drinking or sleeping. What followed was the most disillusioned year of my life. I wandered in and out of relationships and did little else except endure my "iron rice bowl" job.

Then one day, I was asked to conduct a training for the Division of Social Services in California. The woman in charge of training would soon be on maternity leave and they needed a temporary replacement. The training was short, effective, full of humor, and everyone loved it. The division chief happened to be visiting that day, and a few days later, I was told that I would be fast-tracked for a promotion.

The joy from this good news only lasted until I got home. Sitting at home alone, I suddenly realized that if I did accept this promotion, in all likelihood I would stay a government employee forever. I didn't want to spend my life like that. I had more important things to do. Even though the time to realize my dream had not yet come, I could not give it up. If I accepted the promotion, I'd have everything to lose. It would keep me from taking chances. Having nothing to lose is a good thing.

As if arranged by fate, my friend James called from Silicon Valley. He asked me if I would like to join his company and be the manager at the Silicon Valley branch of his technology company.

"You know I know nothing about computers or the Internet. I am not a technology guy."

"We have plenty of tech people. We need people who know everything else. That's where you come in!"

The very next day, I handed in my resignation to my job at the Department of Social Services. I drove north to Silicon Valley, with the Hale-Bopp comet, often called The Great Comet of 1997, guiding me in the California night sky.

I learned a lot during the first year I spent in Silicon Valley. At the end of that year, James asked me if I would like to move to the Beijing office. I accepted. Moving back home to Beijing was wonderful.

However, when I arrived in Beijing, I noticed that the company had really grown. It had gone from a few dozen employees to over six hundred, and it felt like an entirely different animal now. It was difficult for me to understand how, or if, I even fit in anymore. I contemplated leaving my employ at Silicon Valley and making yet another attempt at progressing in the field of psychology.

I thought of Rudy. I wondered if maybe *now* might be a good time for one of his grand plans? I called him and asked if we could meet.

Rudy came on a night train to meet me in Beijing. He told me he now had a better idea. As usual, he was just bursting at the seams to tell me all the details.

I greeted him as he disembarked from the train at the station, but he didn't even break his gait. He slapped a hand on my back and ushered me forward beside him through the throngs gathered on the platform. In one hand, he had a half-dozen papers with names and information about his latest idea. The papers were rolled up in a bundle with a rubber band to secure them. He kept brushing the rubber band off, unfurling them, and flipping through to point

Big, huge *companies are interested in having you give lectures to their employees! Isn't that wonderful? After a couple of lectures, I'm sure other companies will follow.*

at various notations as we walked. He quickly replaced the rubber band snugly when a passerby paused to glance at the papers. He launched a disgusted look over his shoulder, "Nosy!" he said under his breath. I chuckled at his effort to be clandestine.

"Paul, big, *huge* companies are interested in having you give lectures to their employees! Isn't that wonderful? Now we don't have to worry about getting people to come. I already have several companies committed to it. After a couple of lectures, I'm *sure* other companies will follow. This could be the best model to allow this to happen!" He stopped to give me that wide smile. He had opted for contact lenses now, so the thick, black-rimmed glasses were gone. That shock of hair still stuck out at a tilt on the left side. I couldn't say no to Rudy.

The next day, I handed in my resignation at the Silicon Valley company. It was difficult to explain to my mother why I had resigned from a position with good pay and why I had given up on so many stock options.

"I know you don't like it there. But why can't you just stay another year or two and get all your benefits? It's a lot of money!"

"But Mom," I explained, "Rudy has a great plan!"

My mom's eyebrows shot up and she gave me a look of disbelief.

I tried to ease her mind. "Yeah, I know, I know. But maybe this time his plans will work out! I don't know how much time I have left on this earth. I don't want to have regrets."

Saving a Soul

The night before the first lecture, Rudy drove me to the mega-company where I was to speak. I met the CEO of the company and he explained what he wanted.

"Our company has been growing very fast. But competition is fierce. The business environment can be cruel, but that's the way it is. I want my employees to be like hardened soldiers. I want them to be highly self-motivated. When they work, I want them to be like a pack of wild wolves. I want them to have the killer instinct. I want them to be able to work overtime willingly. I want their families to not be holding them back. I want 100% growth annually for the next five years."

In other words, he wanted a motivational speaker on steroids! He didn't want me.

"They just invited the wrong guy. This is not what I am about!" I whisper-shouted to him.

I nudged Rudy and nodded my head toward the hallway door. He followed me out of the room. "They just invited the wrong guy. This is not what I am about!" I whisper-shouted to him.

"But can't you put in some of what he wanted? Mix it in with what you want to talk about?"

"I want to help them become healthier and happier people. He wants them to be wild animals with no human identity!"

"Can't you at least try?" Rudy bit his lower lip and looked at me, unflinching.

I stayed up most of the night trying to make it work. Eventually, I managed to craft a plan and an outline that I thought might be acceptable.

The lecture went well. But when I sat down, the CEO stood up and gave his own speech to wrap up the afternoon. "Let me summarize what we have learned today. Today, we have learned the power of the human psyche. If you think *big*, you can achieve *big*. If you think you're not tired, you will not be tired. If you set high goals, no matter how impossible they may appear to be, you will achieve them! We will build our company like an all-conquering army—on to victory!"

Somehow, he managed to put into his summary not a single concept that I had talked about!

That evening, the CEO brought eight young women to my hotel room. "Mr. Yin, here are eight of the most beautiful young girls in the city. Choose one for yourself!"

"What?" I couldn't believe what he was saying.

"Or you may keep them all! It's up to you!"

"No, I don't need this. Why don't you just let them go home?"

He smiled. "You don't have to be bashful. All right, I will pick one for you. I hope we have similar taste." Then, he picked a very beautiful, young girl and took the rest out of the room.

I sat in my room with the young girl. I looked at her. She looked at me. She was probably under eighteen. She had her hands on her blouse button, waiting for my command.

"Thank you for choosing me."

"You can go home now," I said to her.

"No, I can't leave. Please let me stay."

"What do you mean? Why can't you leave?" I asked.

"Only the one chosen gets paid. That is why I need to stay with you. If I leave right away, then they'd know. They would not pay me."

I thought for a while. "Alright. Then let's talk. How old are you?"

"I'm seventeen."

"Why are you not in school? Why are you doing this for a living? Do your parents know?"

She bit her lips.

"Come on, I want to know."

"I dropped out of school because I'm not good at it. I am doing this so I won't be a burden to my family. I didn't tell my parents, but I think they know. I give them money to help out. I think they can guess but don't really want to know." She looked past me as she spoke.

I moved so that I could look her in the eye. "You think you chose the easy way. But you are wrong. One day you will realize that this seemingly easy beginning will give you a lifetime of pain and regret. You can do better than this."

"But I am not good at anything. I can't do anything else."

"No one at seventeen has work experience. No one at seventeen is good at anything related to work. You get that experience by doing small jobs, starting from the simplest and lowest paying jobs. Then you get better and move up. What you are doing now may seem the easy way. But you will only be seventeen once. Someday you won't be 'the chosen one.' You have a long life ahead. Don't ruin it now."

Tears began to fill her eyes.

"Thank you. No one has ever truly cared for me before." She started to unbutton her blouse.

I told her to stop. "Please don't do that."

"But I want to. You are a wonderful man and, besides, I should earn my payment."

"Listen, you don't owe me. You only owe yourself. Don't you ever forget that."

A slow half-smile spread across her face.

"How long do you have to stay?" I asked.

"Maybe at least two hours."

"Do you want a lecture, or do you want to just chat?"

She laughed and her smile spread to her eyes. "I hate lectures! That's why I dropped out of school! But I actually enjoy talking to you."

We talked for about three hours. Just before she left, she promised me she would find a different job and take responsibility for her own life. I hope she kept her word.

The next morning, Rudy walked into my room with his wide smile. "How was the girl?"

"I sent her home. She will find a different job."

"Hmm . . . she was actually your pay for the lecture," he told me.

"If I saved a soul, that makes it good pay." We both laughed.

"But seriously," I said, "this won't work. They don't want me to talk. They want to use me as a puppet to do their own talking. This is not what I want to do."

> "No!" I said emphatically, "Let's destroy the drawing board!"

"I know." Rudy shook his head in frustration as well. He rubbed his temple with his forefinger. "If I knew it'd be like this, I wouldn't have brought you here. What should we do now? Back to the drawing board?"

"No!" I said emphatically. "Let's destroy the drawing board!"

Recalculating

There's an old Chinese saying which says: "For something to work, you need heaven, earth, and humanity to align." After the experience with the mega-company, I boarded a plane back to the U.S. Things hadn't worked out because none of these three prerequisites were in place. It was time for me to take a step back.

The first person I went to visit in the U.S. was my cousin Joe. Joe was an interesting guy. Whenever anyone asked him something, he'd always smile broadly and nod. On one visit I told him that I was getting married. He smiled and said, "That's nice." About a year later, I told him that I was getting divorced. "That's nice," he said.

That confused me. "How come you say the same thing both times?"

He smiled again. "Because both are things that are supposed to happen. That's why it's nice."

It was almost impossible to get an opinion from this "Smiling Buddha" as his friends liked to call him.

"Paul, you keep saying that China is not ready. That's true." Then he lowered his voice and hit me with some tough questions. "Are *you* ready? Are *you* prepared?"

"I'm beginning to ask myself the same thing," I admitted.

"You're an extremely talented man. You can do almost anything you want. But you have always chosen the path less traveled. That's just you. I don't question the direction you are going." Then he paused. "But for a man with a grand and ambitious plan, have you ever thought that you are not the one who should be doing the planning?"

> *For a man with a grand and ambitious plan, have you ever thought that you are not the one who should be doing the planning?*

I had never really thought of that.

Joe continued. "As noble as your plan appears to be, it is still really egocentric. It's *your* plan. However, you are no more than a speck of dust in the universe. For anything to work in the universe, heaven, earth, and humanity must be aligned.

"The universe is perfect. Do you think it makes sense for the universe to change its plan and all its elements to align just so *your* plan can be realized and *your* dream can come true? Does that make sense at all? You're acting like you want the universe to serve you.

"Get rid of your ego. Get in tune with the universe. When you are truly ready, when the time is right, you will be called. Your assignment will come, along with all the help you'll need. You'll have become a servant rather than a master. You can translate what I say into Christian vocabulary, Buddhist vocabulary, or scientific vocabulary. It doesn't matter what terms you use. That's the truth as I see it."

I thought for a long time about what Joe had said. He was right. What I needed now was not planning or even doing. What I needed was to get myself prepared. I still had a lot to learn. In his Buddhist terms, it was called "cultivation of the self"—making continuous, subtle corrections, adjustments, and improvements, so that you become a better you. I repeatedly contemplated this mantra in my head:

Be patient.

Get rid of the ego.

Be a servant.

Be Buddha-like.

Be Jesus-like.

I decided to start my self-cultivation. I had no specific plan on exactly how long that would take. I decided to leave that to circumstance.

I had to admit I was grieving the loss of Karen. I went to visit a monastery in Los Angeles called the Hsi Lai Temple. This was a place where there was no ego. There was no differentiation, no ambition, and no grand personal plans. It was peaceful there walking alongside the monks and listening to the mysterious, musical chants through the temple walls. But that wasn't why I was there. This sacred land was, ironically, the place where I first went astray.

This was the place where I met Karen. I was taking a class there, but my attention was not on the class. My attention was on Karen who was the most attractive woman in the class. At the time, I thought that taking this fragile young woman under my wing and providing for her was a noble thing. What I didn't realize was that my heart was in a selfish place. I was using her under the guise of generosity to fulfill my own wishes to be her savior.

My "kindness" to her had put her in chains. When I proposed to her, she eventually said yes, not because she wanted to, but because I did so much for her. She owed so much to me that she felt she never had a choice. Her apparent betrayal had hurt me deeply, but did she betray me, or had she simply decided to stop betraying herself?

She came into my life when I needed her, and left when she had become a weight that was pulling me back from my dreams and my mission. Wasn't she the ultimate angel? It was because of my ego that I missed that.

> *Did she betray me, or had she simply decided to stop betraying herself?*

If I did not rid myself of my egocentricity and realize that benevolence was not about me, how could I possibly understand other people without prejudice? How could I help them? There was much work to do in my heart.

Loving the Unloving

As I began my task of self-cultivation, the first thing I knew I needed to do was to change my motivation from self-centered endeavors, however noble they may be, to simple acts of love.

Simple acts of love… that should be easy!

But then, God sent me Mel.

I was an active member of an online classical music forum. One of the most interesting characters on the forum was Mel. He was a lover and defender of the classics and the old masters, and he absolutely hated anything remotely *avant-garde*. Whenever he saw a post about *avant-garde* music, which for him was anything after Schoenberg, he would immediately post a scathing attack on the post and its author.

There were almost never curse words. Instead, it was a hard, and often personal, attack of the highest literary quality, befitting his online alias—The Word Maestro. I became one of his main targets as he trolled me online. Twenty-four hours a day, whenever I'd post, an attack followed within minutes! Did the man ever sleep?

I was angry at first. But anger, I knew, was just the ego's desire to defend itself. Mel seemed to be the perfect gift God had dispatched to help me reign in my ego's selfish needs. I refrained from retaliatory attacks, but he continued for at least six months.

One day, the attacks suddenly stopped. It felt weird. The Word Maestro had suddenly departed. What had happened? A week later, I couldn't hold back my curiosity and asked online if anyone knew of Mel's whereabouts. One person posted that Mel had just been admitted into a hospital for heart surgery. The Medical Center was only about thirty miles from where I lived in California, so I decided to go see him.

When I told the nurses that I was there to see Mel, they all stopped what they were doing to peer at me with furrowed eyebrows. I could tell they were surprised to have a visitor for Mel.

One of the nurses bravely mentioned to me in a hushed tone that Mel had been "somewhat uncooperative." I almost laughed out loud, but I responded by politely telling her that I was well aware that he could be a pretty lousy jerk.

One day, the attacks suddenly stopped . . . The Word Maestro had suddenly departed. What happened?

She exhaled and shook her head. "We really need your help. He is just impossible! We don't know what to do! He's refusing treatment!"

I followed her around the nurses' station through the brightly-lit hall.

She knocked lightly outside of room 214. "Mel, there's someone here to see you."

"Tell whoever that joker is to go away! I have no family or friends! Tell 'em to get the hell out!" he blasted.

I walked past the nurse and stood by his bedside. "After all these months of attacking me, don't you want to be able to attack me to my face?" I stuck out my hand. "Hello, Word Maestro. I'm SpringRite."

He was sitting upright in the hospital bed with a labyrinth of tubes and wires looping in and out of his hospital garment. He looked at me, confused. *"You* are *SpringRite?"* He did not reach for my hand.

"The one and only!" I showed my teeth to make a smile shape on my face.

Mel was stunned. "Why are you here? Why have you come to see me?"

"I'm here because you are a devoted lover of great music, and I love you for that. I heard about the difficulties you're having, and I'm here to support you." I lowered my hand. I stood awkwardly next to the bed with the rail separating us.

Mel closed his eyes tightly. He sat there like that for a minute. He started to look angry, and I began to question my decision to come. I suddenly wasn't sure if I was actually prepared to handle more character assassination from the Word Maestro.

He was indeed angry, but he was angry at himself. Tears started seeping out of his tightly closed eyes. He placed his thumbs on his jaw and spread his fingers along his forehead loosely covering his face, "Why did I attack you like that? Why? You're supposed to hate me. But here you are, trying to help not only a stranger, but a stranger who has been mercilessly attacking you for months!" He couldn't control the flow of tears now; he peered at me with glassy red eyes.

I handed him a tissue from the bedside table. "Attacking me? Those were just words. They mean nothing to me. But your passions moved me. Your brilliant attacks impressed me! I always wanted to get to know you. When I heard you were only a few miles away, I wasn't going to give up this opportunity." I hugged him. His body shook with emotion.

"Listen. You really should leave. The truth is I don't want to live anymore. I don't want to go through the operation. It's not worth it. I've suffered enough, and I want it to stop now. Let me go, please. Allow me to give up."

The nurses had informed me that Mel had multiple problems. But, if he went through a specific surgery on his heart, his prognosis was actually quite good. I said, "Mel, I haven't listened attentively to much Wagner for a while. I want to listen to Wagner with his most devoted fan. I also want an opportunity to torture you with some Alban Berg and Boulez. I want to get to know you. I want to know about how you grew up. We have lots of things we need to do together. I know this is a difficult time for you right now, but I'm here now. And I want to help."

Mel looked me in the eye and bit his upper lip. Then he relented, "Okay, SpringRite. Just for you, I'll try."

I smiled at the nurses on my way out. "Mel should be better now," I said.

The surgery went fine, but two days after the operation, I got a phone call in the middle of the night informing me that Mel had disappeared from his hospital room. Since I was the only visitor on record, I was the next phone call they made after calling the police.

"Give me his address!" I implored.

"His address? What do you mean? His house is three hundred miles away in Las Vegas!" The nurse on the other end of the line was clearly confused about why I wanted his home address.

"I can guarantee he's heading to his home in Las Vegas. He has decided to give up. But he doesn't want to die in a hospital. He wants to die at home while listening to Wagner! That's where he is heading!"

"But what can we do, Mr. Yin?"

"I'm driving to Las Vegas to find him. I want you to contact a hospital there to get ready to receive a patient who just had heart surgery. I will get him into the hospital one way or another. I'll contact you in about six hours."

I grabbed a recording of *St. Mathew's Passion* by J. S. Bach and Wagner's *Gotterdammerung*. I headed east on I-15.

Five hours later, I knocked on Mel's door. I knocked for a couple of minutes. Finally, clad in just his pajama pants, Mel flung the door open. "For the love of—!" Mel couldn't believe what he was seeing. "Wha—how did you know I would be here? How did you find my place?"

"God told me. Let me help you." I walked past him and helped myself to a seat on the sofa. I motioned for him to return to what was the lone chair in the corner where he had obviously been lounging just moments before. We sat down and looked at each other. We both had tears in our eyes. Neither could speak past the lumps in our throats.

Mel finally broke the silence, "I'm weak, Paul." He cupped his left hand in a ball and put his knuckle to his mouth. "I can't do this anymore. I'm giving up. But I can't die without my Wagner. *Gotterdammerung!*"

Tears welled up in my eyes and threatened to spill over. I blinked them away. "Mel, what are you doing? The surgery was successful. The most critical times are the first few days after surgery. You just got through that. We were winning!

"Why are you here?" he asked again.

"You are not leaving this world until you become a believer in human compassion and love."

"But I absolutely refuse to go back to the hospital! Never again!" Mel insisted.

I took a look at Mel sitting there in his pajamas. He looked so small and vulnerable. He was such a bitter man, with wit so sharp that he could eviscerate the noblest sage. This powerful, proud man sat in front of me, just a waif with no will to live. He was like a little puddle.

> *He was such a bitter man, with wit so sharp that he could eviscerate the noblest sage. This powerful, proud man sat in front of me, just a waif with no will to live.*

I thought for a minute. "Mel," I said, "what if we make your apartment into a hospital ward?"

He inhaled deeply and responded with an almost imperceptible nod of his head.

I made arrangements with the local hospital. I also hired three custodians to clean Mel's apartment and turn it into a sparkling clean hospital ward. The hospital sent equipment and a nurse. Mel could do his recovery at home now.

I posted a notice to the music forum on his behalf which explained his condition and encouraged those who knew him to drop him an encouraging line. Twenty to thirty cards started to show up in Mel's mailbox each day! This man, who was once so cynical, was now swimming in a sea of love.

One day, Mel explained why he had become so embittered. "Paul, you said you wanted me to believe in human compassion and love. I knew those things when I was young. I had a high school sweetheart. After high school, we went to the same college and took the same courses for four years. We were the perfect couple. Everyone envied us. We were planning to be married after graduation, but just before the wedding, she died in a car accident."

Mel stopped. His eyes filled with tears. "I loved her so much; I decided never to enter into a relationship with another woman and never to get married. I kept my word." Then he said, "I had been so content with my life. I became a high school teacher and a baseball umpire. But slowly I changed. I then became abrasive and cynical. She wouldn't have liked to see this side of me." Then Mel turned to me, "Paul, maybe she's the one who sent you?"

"If so, I am glad she called upon me. I am honored."

"Paul, you went miles out of your way just to help a stranger. I must honor that. I won't give up now."

Two years later, Mel needed a second surgery at the California hospital. He didn't want to bother, but I insisted that he go.

"Mel, it's the seventh inning stretch and we are winning five to zero. Even a grand slam wouldn't beat us. This is no time to throw in the towel!"

"But I don't know how to get there," he launched his excuse.

"I'll drive to Las Vegas to pick you up. We'll return to LA. After the surgery, I'll drive you back and we will make your home a hospital ward again, just like last time."

"But that's twenty hours of driving! That's crazy!" He launched his second excuse, but I was ready.

"I have never listened to sixteen hours of *The Ring* all the way through. I will bring the CDs. We will listen together. Remember, you made a pledge to do that, and you haven't done it yet. This is your chance!" Since Mel had no more excuses, he agreed to my plan.

A few months later, Mel invited me to Las Vegas and treated me to the VIP suite in a Las Vegas hotel. He introduced me to everyone as "the man who made me believe in humanity." But I actually believed Mel was sent to me by God. In my self-cultivation, I needed an important lesson, and Mel was the teacher. We all have love within us. But for most of us, love is also a selfish thing.

I thought about the tendency of people to reserve love for themselves, their family members, friends, people they like, and people who like them back. The Chinese have a saying, "The tears of a stranger are just water." In all these cases, there are personal benefits to loving someone. But benevolence is on another plane. It no longer differentiates or discriminates. It is love for all.

> *We all have love within us. But for most of us, love is also a selfish thing.*

To get to this level, I realized I first had to get rid of my ego. Then, I had to get rid of the need to judge. When I learned to love the people who disliked me, people whom I used to dislike, and people who were unfriendly or even hurtful toward me, then I was on a path to being more Buddha-like. I was on a path to being more Jesus-like. I was beginning to possibly qualify as God's helper or God's agent—an agent of love. I was opening my heart to true joy.

That time in the VIP suite in Las Vegas was the very last time I saw Mel. Two years later, he had a foot amputated. He took it well and sent me a photo of himself smiling at the camera while on crutches. But on July 16, 2009, he passed away in his home while holding the remote control in his hand. He died without suffering, watching a Wagnerian opera. That was just the way he had wanted it. This was his final message to me just four months before he passed away:

I'm not too well. In fact, on Tuesday I'm going back to the medical center in California for a series of CAT scans on my spine and abdominal organs. I have my fingers crossed. But I'm not too optimistic. I'm almost seventy-three and my body is worn out. But hope springs eternal. I'll let you know what the outcome is. Meanwhile, take care of your family.

You are a true friend. And I will never forget you.

~Mel

I will never forget you either.

CHAPTER 5

AIRBORNE

I celebrate myself,
And what I assume, you shall assume,
For every atom belonging to me as good belongs to you.
~Walt Whitman, Leaves of Grass

Return to China

In 2002, I was almost thirty-nine and had been living in the U.S. for twenty-two years. I felt ready to go back to Beijing where I was born.

The Americans in California called me Chinese. The Chinese in Beijing called me American. I never took these labels seriously. I was neither and I was both. I was still a Chinese citizen. I had yet to file my U.S. citizenship application. Citizenship meant little to me–Chinese or American. Isn't being a citizen of earth enough? Isn't being a member of mankind enough? Isn't being the son of every man, the brother of every woman, or the father of every child enough?

I felt I had learned my lessons from the past. I now knew that I needed to tame my enthusiasm and be patient. I don't make the call: I answer the call.

November 1, 2002, was the day I would return to Beijing. November second was my parents' wedding anniversary. And since my green card status dictated that I could not be away from the U.S. for more than six months during any twelve-month period, I also booked a return ticket back to California for April 30. That return date proved to have immense significance on my future path in life.

I spent almost six months reuniting with family and friends, and I enjoyed reconnecting with my beloved Beijing.

Just ten days before I was scheduled to leave China, the television news reporters revealed that Beijing had officially become the center of the greatest viral epidemic in decades. Severe Acute Respiratory Syndrome (SARS) was ravaging the city. SARS was an airborne virus that could be contracted through just casual contact with an infected person. And since it was a virus, antibiotics were ineffective as treatment. Upon diagnosis, people were quarantined from the public. There was no cure, and people were quickly dying. As unlikely and improbable as it was, I was there, right in the center of it. But I had my ticket out in ten days.

Was it strange that I would be in Beijing on that day? What did it signify? Was this mere coincidence?

In any case, with the scourge of SARS ravaging the city, there seemed to be only one sensible decision—leave the city. There was indeed a mass exodus. Panic-stricken people were leaving, legally and illegally; if not for a foreign country, then certainly for a safer part of China. There I sat, ticket in hand, but my stomach was churning. Was my soul demanding that I chart a different course? One that seemed like nonsense to any rational person?

I couldn't sleep that night.

I got up. I went to my chair. I sat quietly. I listened to my soul.

Pascal has said, "All men's troubles derive from his inability to sit quietly in a room alone."

I had never felt so troubled. I sat there quietly for many hours, until I noticed the first ray of sunlight.

As I walked outside at five in the morning, I knew my calling had come. It was time to answer the call. I must stay. I must help. But what about my parents? As if my free-spiritedness, my individualism, my single life, the lack of a grandchild, and the fact that I had always chosen eccentricity over pragmatism had not burdened them enough. They both had high blood pressure. Mom had broken her spine four times. Would my decision to stay and contribute my little part in this epic battle put too much stress on them? Could they accept my decision?

Having lived alone most of my life, I had never had to consult parents, wife, in-laws, or other relatives. When I saw a path that I deemed right, I'd take it. Life was nothing but a series of decisions. Different decisions lead to different experiences and different consequences. My decision that day had actually been made many years before. But it had lain dormant, like a seed in the desert, waiting for the first drop of rain. This was my opportunity to give back to my country. I was going to stay, despite the danger and my reservations.

While most people saw SARS as a huge medical issue, SARS itself only infected a few thousand people. But fear and helplessness gripped the nation. From the quarantined patients and their families, to medical workers and their families, to the families of those who unfortunately might die from the virus, they were all people who needed help. I knew I *must* stay. It was my calling.

> *Fear and helplessness gripped the nation. From the quarantined patients and their families, to medical workers and their families, to the families of those who unfortunately might die from the virus, they were all people who needed help.*

I thought of Tia, one of my dad's former students, who now worked at a radio station in Beijing. I gave her a call to entreat her assistance with what had been lain on my heart.

"Hi, this is Mr. Yin's son, Paul. Do you remember me?" I asked.

"Of course, I will never forget you singing opera when you were just a child! How old are you now?" she asked.

"I am forty. Can you believe it? I must have been ten when we last met."

"Right! I think I was maybe fifteen at that time. What are you doing in town?" she asked.

I let her know that I was just visiting and I had my ticket to go back to the U.S. on April 30th.

"Well, thank God! Get out as soon as you can. It is even more dangerous in this city than you think! It is unbelievable! Leave!" she said.

"But Tia, I want to stay. I could use your help," I said calmly.

"Stay? Why?" She sounded both puzzled and concerned. "This is no time for heroism. Get out now!"

> *The biggest enemy is fear. It is psychological. A lot of people need psychological intervention. But this is not well recognized here in China. There are very few experienced professionals.*

"Listen, I am a psychologist. The biggest enemy is fear. It is psychological. A lot of people need psychological intervention. But this is not well recognized here in China. There are very few experienced professionals, but I am one," I explained.

"You don't have to do this!"

"If a fireman was taking his family for a vacation, and as he was leaving the house he saw the house across the street on fire, what would he do? If he continued to the airport, then he should forever quit his profession! He just lost his right to be a firefighter! If I were already in Los Angeles, then you would be right; I wouldn't be obligated to fly in. However, I'm already here! And I know my experience and expertise is needed. I have a duty to stay."

Tia went quiet. Then, her voice began to crack. "Paul, honestly. Ugh . . . okay. You are such a wonderful soul. As a friend, I want you to leave. But if it is your decision to stay, I'll do everything I can to help you. What can I do?"

"I need to contact the Ministry of Health, the Center for Disease Control, the mayor's office, and all the SARS-designated hospitals. I know you can find the right contacts for me, please!" I pleaded.

Tia was fast. The very next day, I had several phone numbers. I called the Ministry of Health twice. I suggested that psychological support and counseling needed to be intensified. The available phone hotlines were not enough. We shouldn't wait for those who need help to find us. We should reach out to them and deliver the services proactively. Most importantly, I suggested that there should be at least one psychological counselor *on-site* at every SARS treatment center for the medical workers, and if needed, for the patients as well. There should also be counselors at the quarantined places and for the patients' and medical workers' families. If someone should die from SARS, psychological intervention for the family should be made available.

To my surprise, they really seemed to like my ideas. I offered to go anyplace, any time to help since I was trained in psychology and had experience in counseling. I told them that I had a ticket to return to the U.S. on the 30th of the month, but would certainly stay if they could use my volunteer services.

They took down my phone number and email address. If they called me before my plane departed, I'd stay. If they contacted me via email after I have left and told me that I was needed here, I would fly back.

Then I called the Beijing Center for Disease Control and several other places. We had brief conversations, and I left my phone number as a potential volunteer on call. I could hear from their hoarse voices and the background noises that they were overwhelmed and were working hard. At the end of every call, I thanked them for their great work.

Later, I tested several hotlines. I heard nothing but busy signals at all the hotlines for over half an hour. That was the problem with phone hotlines. They helped many people. That part is true. But even if the lines weren't always busy, someone had to actually call. In addition, they did not help severe cases.

Most people in China who suffer from severe stress and anxiety do not seek help. They lock themselves up. When they do gather enough courage to make that phone call, the busy signal usually discourages them. More often than not, it also heightens their anxiety level. After a few fruitless attempts, they hang up and never call again.

I knew I had to find another way to reach out to those who needed help.

It was early in the morning on April 28th. My plane would depart in forty-eight hours.

I sat at my desk and wrote a letter which described my recommendations for training and reaching out. In my letter I explained that those who were quarantined may suffer from depression, and those who had family members infected may also suffer from depression and Post Traumatic Stress Disorder (PTSD).

I had made up my mind. I was staying in Beijing.

When I informed my parents of my decision, they didn't try to talk me out of it. Instead, they were both understanding and supportive.

However, injecting myself into this crisis as a properly trained mental health caregiver proved to be more difficult than I thought. Everything in China is organized around "The Unit" sanctioned by the government (work, school, study, or organizational affiliation). It would be difficult for me to get inside the system.

I was frustrated that I hadn't heard back from any of the agencies I contacted, but I went to the airport anyway to return my plane ticket.

"I need to return this ticket to Los Angeles," I told the ticket agent.

"No. You're crazy. I have hundreds of people on the waiting list just for a ticket like this. Also, you do realize there will be a service charge and you will only get two-thirds of the money back," he informed me.

"That will be perfectly all right," I said.

He suddenly looked up. His mouth fell slightly open. "Why are you returning your ticket?"

"I am staying as a volunteer to fight SARS," I replied.

He furrowed his eyebrows and inspected me more closely with a tilt of his head, then he excused himself and disappeared in the back room. He returned with an approving smile. "Thank you for what you are doing. I've been approved to give you a full refund! Good luck and stay safe!"

Entering the War Zone

The worst thing about statistics is that they threaten to turn every human drama into a series of numbers. In a war, those not at the battlefield hear about attrition, neutralization, residual damage, and casualties. What are they? Just numbers. If we want small ones, then we can say *two* enemy divisions were effectively neutralized. If we want large numbers, then we can say enemy attrition was in the *tens of thousands*. But large or small, they are just numbers. What's more, they are far away. We don't see the faces, nor do we feel the anguish, hear the cries, taste the blood, or smell the stench of death.

> *Beijing was now a War Zone. Everyone inside the city knew it. How did we know? We knew it through numbers.*

SARS smashed into Beijing like an asteroid. Although we didn't hear explosions or smell gunpowder, Beijing was now a War Zone. Everyone inside the city knew it. How did we know? We knew it through numbers. For more than a week, we daily confirmed new cases ranging from 100 to 160 in addition to a slightly higher number of daily "suspected cases."

As of May 5th, 2003, more than 15,000 people were under quarantine. As there were 20,000,000 people who were residents of the city, it wasn't a high percentage, but the numbers were large enough and growing steadily enough to alert even the calmest of souls. I was among the calm. But even I must admit to having felt anxiety in those moments.

Every day at four o'clock, people stopped everything to listen to the latest daily numbers of deaths as released by the Ministry of Health.

One day I turned on the TV dutifully at four o'clock. Good news. The numbers for the two days prior were 96 and 112 respectively, down from the previous week when they were close to 150 a day. Today's number was 69, the lowest since the numbers started to be released. The measures taken by the government, medical community, and communities in general seemed to be taking effect. I took a deep breath as if to celebrate the knowledge that there were now fewer viruses in the air.

A quick check of the refrigerator told me a trip to the grocery store was in order. I put on a long-sleeved shirt and a mask and headed for the elevator.

The grocery store was less than a block away. There was a buying frenzy there just two weeks ago. Everything on the shelves was bought up due to rumors of martial law and severe shortages. But it stopped when the government quickly dispelled the rumors and restocked the stores. In the days following the government's announcement, everything had been calmer.

As I walked toward the grocery store through the beautiful streets of my beloved Beijing, I saw a SARS ambulance zoom by. It stopped at the apartment complex next to the store. Two medical workers stepped out of the back of the ambulance in their heavy, multi-layered SARS gear, looking like astronauts.

Throughout the SARS epidemic I had kept medical field notes, and the sight of the driver of that ambulance haunted me so much that I recorded this entry:

The driver sits in the front seat, dressed in full germ gear. The only parts of her features visible are her eyes. She sits there like a statue, holding the steering wheel with one hand and the gear stick with the other, ready to zoom off as soon as the patient is brought down. After about a minute, she suddenly shakes her head violently. I realize that she is shaking off the sweat that is about to enter her eyes. She resumes her ready position. There is a look of determination in her eyes. If I could see her feet, I would see that one is already planted firmly on the gas pedal. She knows the importance of her job. She's determined to perform her job to its utmost perfection as if God had personally given her this assignment.

A few minutes later, the patient is brought out. He looks extremely ill. The small crowd along the street backs off. The patient is placed in the back of the ambulance. Once the patient is secured, the ambulance takes off.

Tomorrow's number may go up by one. But this *one* is not just another *one*.

This *one* is from *my* neighborhood. This *one* has a face. In fact, this *one* has many faces: the face of the patient himself, the barber who cut his hair two days ago, the taxi driver who drove him home three days ago, his wife whom he tried to convince last night that he just had a cold or one too many cigarettes, his daughter who called the ambulance, all the residents in the building who had been sharing the same elevator, all the people who work or shop at the grocery store where he shops every day, the two medical people who went in to get him, and most memorably, the *one* who has the face of the ambulance driver.

If tomorrow's number is only one, will I think that it is a small number? Will any of the people who were there, or any of the people I mentioned above, think it is a small number? Any one?

There is only *one* number, and the number is *one. For every atom belonging to me as good belongs to you.*

I Wait

Several days had passed and I still hadn't heard back from any of the agencies I had contacted. One of my acquaintances did call to tell me that my chances of getting in anywhere were slim at best. "You have to have a 'unit,' you know. You must be part of a government-sanctioned group. Or at least, you must be a 'real Chinese.' They see you as an American. They don't trust you."

Isn't it funny that I am only seen as Chinese outside of China?

But I slowly started to work on my own. A friend of my parents called about a neighbor who was having panic attacks. I went. Another had a daughter called to work on the front line, directly with infected patients. The family, especially the mother, was suffering severe anxiety attacks. Again, I went. They referred me to other families of front line medical workers. I made a couple of house calls each day. It was a start.

However, I still came up against many walls. I started visiting some community centers and neighborhood committees. At one community center, the person in charge told me that she knew of several people in the neighborhood suffering from anxiety. They had locked themselves up in their own homes with several months' supply of instant noodles. She asked me what I would suggest.

"If you can get their phone numbers, I can call them and talk to them."

"Oh, that would be wonderful! We are all afraid some harm might come to them. There are already reports of people having committed suicide because of the fear. I will just need to ask some of my higher-ups."

Okay. "I can also give a few small classes on stress management. If you can get a room and make the announcement on the bulletin board, people who need it can come."

"Oh, that would be great! I think we can get a classroom from the school or the kindergarten. We can have a morning class and an afternoon class this weekend . . . Of course, I will need to ask some of my higher-ups."

Here we go again.

Finally, I got a positive phone call. A hospital wanted to talk to me. The next morning I hailed a taxi and got in. Like all taxis in Beijing, the windows were rolled down, but still I could smell the disinfectant chemicals. The driver wore a thick face mask.

"Where would you like to go?" he asked.

"To the hospital."

The driver suddenly became nervous. "Are you a patient going to the SARS center? In that case, you are supposed to call the SARS ambulance."

"No, I am not. Please don't be nervous. I am going for work-related matters."

"I see."

He did not seem to believe me. But business was slow. He stepped on the gas.

Beijing cab drivers are famous, or *in*famous, for being overly talkative. In fact, Beijingers as a "class" of people are famous for being chatty, but we talked very little on the way. The SARS virus was spreading through the air. The best defense seemed to be everyone keeping his or her mouth shut.

Twenty minutes later, we arrived at the hospital gate. I looked at the meter. It read twenty-four Renminbi (RMB). I took my wallet out.

The driver again asked me, "Why are you coming here? Can you tell me?"

"I guess you can say I'm here to beg them to let me go to the front line to help in this fight. I'm a typical Beijinger. I cannot sit at home when I know Beijing needs me."

He turned around in his seat to look at me, and then he said calmly, "No, don't pay me. Today's ride is free."

What? I was confused. "But I must pay you. Business is down. I heard all cab drivers are working at a loss every day."

He looked at me. "Sir, I'm a simple man. I don't have any skills. The only skill I have is that I know how to drive. I want so badly to be able to contribute to this war against SARS! But I can't do anything. Do you know how frustrating that is? If you go in there, and they accept your request to go to the front, then, by being the one to drove you here for free, I will have contributed in a miniscule way to this fight. It is the only way that I can contribute."

He wiped his cheek with the back of his hand as he turned and looked back toward his steering wheel. "All right. I thank you."

"No, I thank *you!*" He sniffed and put both hands back at ten and two.

Team ONE

I was met outside the hospital by a Mr. Cheung, an assistant to the hospital administrator. It was too risky to let me in to the hospital, he told me.

"What's the risk?" I asked.

His eyes darted toward the hospital. "Let's just meet at a coffee shop down the street. You do deserve a candid explanation."

Most of the restaurants in Beijing were closed due to the fear of spreading SARS. Those that were open had limited business. The most famous restaurant in Beijing, the Quanjude Peking Duck Restaurant, remained open, but business was down ninety percent. The only place that was still doing a brisk business was the take-out window at Kentucky Fried Chicken. No one was out and about on the normally bustling streets. No one wanted to have anyone too close. If they thought someone was too close for comfort, they'd just cough. People would scatter away.

We decided to meet at a coffee shop in the middle of town. It had outdoor patio seating. Mr. Cheung was about my age. He had smooth, healthy skin and a slender, athletic build. He extended his hand, and we shook.

"I do appreciate your effort and thank you for meeting me to discuss this further," I said.

He shook his head and began to apologize, but paused while we ordered a couple of lattes.

He began again. "I really am sorry, Mr. Yin. I know you think psychological intervention is very much needed today. Personally, I totally agree with you. But there are several problems. First, from the leadership and hospital management's points of view, the medical aspect of this epidemic takes on a much higher priority. We are already overwhelmed on that front as it is.

"Secondly, you came from America. You are from outside the *house* so to speak. If we use you, and someone from higher-up finds out about it, we may be in trouble. It's not so much that the higher-ups may disapprove. In the Chinese culture, you just don't make decisions over the head of someone higher up, even if your decision is correct. This is the risk I was referring to. Finally, the people who need you–I specifically mean the medical workers who are under enormous stress—don't think they need you and are trying to handle it on their own just like they've always been told. This is the Chinese Way, or…"

He paused to savor a sip of his latte. "Or they are afraid that someone will know that they went to talk to a psychologist. Just the thought is more frightening to them than the fright and the stress they are facing."

> *You came from America. You are from outside* the house *so to speak. If we use you, and someone from higher-up finds out about it, we may be in trouble.*

"On the way over here, I was thinking about this," I said. "I should have known this. In fact, I do know this. For some reason, maybe because of my enthusiasm, I somehow forgot. This is China. I'm dealing with the Chinese culture."

Mr. Cheung explained further that many assumed the problem was political. He said that there *are* political aspects to it, but for the most part, the problem was cultural. This is a culture where decisions have always come from the top. He pointed out that it is just as true in the family as it is in the nation. Mr. Cheung did seem to have his finger on the pulse. I wasn't surprised to learn that this was what I was up against.

Mr. Cheung went inside to get a second latte while I thought over what he had said.

When he came back, I asked, "Can you give me a clear picture on the psychological states of your medical staff on the front line, or of those about to go?"

"Well, it's hard to generalize. Most of them are fine, or at least most of them seem fine. But some are obviously stressed. We have one nurse who suffered a complete mental breakdown. We had to have her protected."

"You mean locked up."

"I didn't use that word. I said *protected,*" he reiterated. "We'll send a psychiatrist from the psychiatric hospital to treat her."

"What do you know about the families?"

"I think the families are more stressed than the medical workers or the patients. They are the ones who need you more than anyone."

"Can you help me to get to them?"

He thought it over for a long time.

"I can, technically, but I don't think I should. If I refer you to ten of them, and one is offended by the offer, it could be a big problem for me."

"Has anyone mentioned to you that they would like to have some psychological support?"

"Yes, a couple of head nurses have requested help for the nurses under them. I have reported that to the higher-ups. Hopefully they will send someone through their official channels."

"What do you see as the number one problem for the medical staff on the front line?"

"Every day they work six hours directly with those infected, sometimes more. The working conditions are challenging. They wear three layers of protective suits plus three masks. It is hot, stuffy, and impossible to breathe. If they need to go to the restroom, or if they need a drink of water, it takes thirty minutes to get out of the suits and then get back in. So, they don't drink water for at least an hour prior to starting their shifts, and they don't drink water until they finish the shift. That is six to eight hours with no food, no drink, and no bathroom breaks. They wear adult diapers to make it through.

"The work is also perilous. As of now, there are more than three hundred medical workers in Beijing infected. Lately, we have cut the rate of infection among medical workers to just a few a day. Hopefully, we can cut it to zero."

"What about after work?"

"I was just going to talk about that. After six hours of enormous stress and discomfort, the rest of the time is filled with utter boredom. Even though we have very strict procedures to protect them, it's still possible that someone may be infected. To prevent potential cross-contamination among the medical workers, after work they pretty much stay on their own, each in his or her own room. They can't go home. They can't go out."

"So, the day contains these two extremes." I was beginning to see a clear picture.

"Yes. That's not easy to deal with."

"I see."

"Did they all volunteer to go to the front line, or were they ordered to go there?"

I sensed I had hit a nerve when he did not respond..

> *Did they all volunteer to go to the front line, or were they ordered to go there?*

After a long pause, he said, "Well, that depends on how you look at it. Technically, everyone signed up to go."

"Technically? Do you mean some might have been ordered to go?"

"No, at least not in my hospital. I can assure you that most of them did, in fact, volunteer. But I know there are some who were disinclined."

"When they see everyone around them sign up, don't you think they also feel pressured to sign up?" I asked.

"You're right," he conceded, "it is peer pressure. We are a collective, conformist society, you know. These are the people who might potentially have psychological problems."

I just shook my head.

"Have you heard about that doctor who disappeared?" Mr. Cheung asked me. "He had a patient who had SARS-like symptoms, so the doctor just got up and left the hospital. The patient thought he went to the restroom. Three days later, the hospital called his home and it turned out that the doctor went to England ending his career as a doctor forever."

We talked on and on for nearly three hours.

Finally, Mr. Cheung looked down at the table and shook his head. "Unfortunately, Mr. Yin, the truth is that we can't get you inside."

"Then I will work on the outside."

He laughed.

"You are just like they said you would be!"

"They? Who are they?"

"Someone I know from across the Pacific. You've got a reputation, you know." He smiled.

"I will work as a team of one," I said.

Mr. Cheung shook my hands. "Paul, please don't think you are a team of one. There are many people who support what you are doing. You may seem to be a team of one, but you are a team of many. There are invisible people behind you and around you. I am a supporter of the Liverpool football club. We have a song. Just remember the title."

I was also a fan. I also knew the song. We spoke the title in one voice: "You'll Never Walk Alone!"

A Mother's Love

That evening and the following morning, I contacted every medical worker or family that I knew, as well as some reporters. I told them to give me the information and I would do the work. We gave our team a distinctive name: ONE. That afternoon, I got my first case. I received a call from a doctor on the front line. It was only her second day on the job. She was panicking.

"Mr. Yin, I can't do this. I am thinking about running away from my duties. I'm getting out!" I could hear the fear in her voice.

She admitted to me that she felt extremely unsafe dealing with SARS patients, but she felt that she couldn't walk away from her job. If she did, her career would be ruined forever, and her own eight-year-old daughter would live with a shadow over her for the rest of her life.

"I can hear that you feel afraid. Have you ever been afraid as a doctor before?" I asked.

"No, not like this. I simply can't do it anymore. Please don't think I'm weak. I'm being honest. I only have ten minutes to try to get away. I am expected to get suited for a new patient, an eight-year-old little girl. I have to leave *now*!"

It was obvious that she was not in the best state of mind to perform her duties. However, if she ran away, it would be against Chinese professional ethics. She'd probably pay a heavy price for it. Her worries about what it might do to her daughter were real as well. I was not a "political thought correction worker." I couldn't make decisions for her. But I needed to find a way to get a better outcome—the best possible outcome. I suddenly remembered her description of this new patient.

Since she only had ten minutes before her new patient came in, I asked her to consider waiting until after she treated this one patient before she made such a monumental decision to run away. I told her I would gladly have a lengthy discussion with her as soon as she finished treating her patient.

After a few seconds of silence, she said, "And you promise you will answer my call?"

I promised.

"Do you have any advice for me right now about how to handle today's case?"

"Yes. But first, let me ask you a simple question. Who are you?"

"Who am I? What do you mean?"

"What is the first thing that comes to mind?"

"I'm a doctor."

"True. But you're also a mother. Now, I want you to go back in there not as a doctor, but as a mother. Think like a mother. Talk like a mother. Act like a mother. Be a mother."

She didn't call back that night, but one day, after the SARS crisis was over, she called and told me what happened. She said when she went in she truly saw that little girl, who was about the same age as her own daughter and looked quite a bit like her daughter.

> *Now, I want you to go back in there not as a doctor, but as a mother. Think like a mother. Talk like a mother. Act like a mother. Be a mother.*

Struggling for breath, the little girl looked up at her and asked, "Am I going to die, Doctor?"

She looked into the girl's eyes and said, "No, sweetheart, you won't. I will take care of you. While you are in here, I will be your mother. A mother would never allow her child to die while under her care. I will protect you. I promise."

Suddenly, the motherly instinct in her was awakened. She became calm and brave. She was still afraid, but she was able to perform her doctor's duties beautifully. Afterwards, she decided to be a mother to all her patients, regardless of age or gender. She overcame her fear. There is no stronger love or stronger will than that of a mother.

Things Learned

In small ways I was able to continue to counsel others in need throughout the SARS epidemic, and thankfully it was all over faster than expected. Credit must be given to the government as well as all the medical professionals from across the country for eradicating the virus. What I could do was rather limited. However, I had learned a lot about how the system works. Most importantly, I learned much about the changing Chinese culture and its people.

After the SARS odyssey ended, my plan to stay in China long-term was a done deal. My green card had become invalid because of my overstaying in China. I had to reapply if wanted to go back. Countless people advised me to do exactly that. A couple of attorneys assured me that it would be no problem at all. But now, I was determined to stay. First, as my parents grew older, they would need their son close by. It would be time to assume my filial duties. More importantly, after the two unsuccessful attempts to launch my mental health project in China, and after patiently waiting and getting myself prepared, the time for this launch appeared to have finally arrived.

During the SARS crisis, the Chinese experienced a psychological crisis first hand. That would make them much more open to accepting psychological intervention, or at least mental health education. I was not about to abandon that opening for a residence card that didn't carry a lot of significance to me. It was time to grab the bull by the horns and move forward.

Chapter 6

A STAR IS BORN

Focus on purpose, not on outcome. Focus on it at home or in your work, with love as your one and only motivation, and you will have superhuman strength and energy. It gives everything meaning. It makes you a winner instantly. Best of all, the universe seems to go into synchronicity mode and conspires to help you.
~Paul Yin, "Newsletter"

The Ying to my Yang

As 2004 approached, God threw me in an unexpected direction which had nothing to do with my goal to bring the field of psychology to China. Or so I thought.

I was asked to attend a dinner in Beijing where several Canadian education officials would be present. At that dinner, I met Vanessa, the assistant to the Canadian principal at the school. We exchanged telephone numbers for networking purposes, but somehow, when I tucked her card in my pocket, I knew I would not be calling her only about business.

Prior to that exchange, while I was knee-deep in a conversation with another administrator, her eye had caught mine. In that moment, a picture of her standing next to me in my old age had flashed through my mind. I scoffed at my brain for allowing myself to be distracted, but I couldn't shake that image after I returned home.

A few weeks later, I pulled the card from my wallet. "Hello, Vanessa. This is Paul. Do you remember me? We met at a dinner a while back," I said.

"Oh yes, I do remember . . .," she said in a weak voice.

"How have you been?"

"I'm, uh, a little sick." Her voice had the unmistakable skips in timbre that told me she was suffering from laryngitis.

"I am sorry to hear that. Have you had dinner?"

"No. I am debating whether to call for pizza or just go to sleep. Or, I think I may have some instant noodle..."

I saw an opening to woo her with my nurturing spirit and culinary skills, so I told her not to bother. I would be right there.

When I arrived, Vanessa was in bed, and she definitely had a fever. I checked her temperature, put a wet towel on her head, then headed for the kitchen. Thirty minutes later, I had prepared soup and a four-course meal.

I left right after washing the dishes and cleaning the kitchen.

My plan was successful. We began to see each other daily. Before I knew it, we were in love.

It's hard to explain what we saw in each other. We had nothing in common other than being close in age. Vanessa is an uncomplicated woman. She's beautiful, kind, honest, direct, and hangs her heart on her sleeve. She always says what she means and, if she's unhappy about something, she always lets me know. There is no guesswork with her. I like that.

My friends thought I should at least find someone with a higher education degree. Her friends thought she should find someone with some money or at least a practical guy who had a job! But neither one of us seemed bothered by these sentiments.

We were two people with no apparent interest in marriage whatsoever who had met almost by accident. Personally, I had given up on marriage, not because of my previously failed marriage, but because I thought my endeavors would be a burden on family life. I didn't make much money. I was not practical. I liked the road less traveled.

We had opposite personalities, no common interests, totally different lives with circles of friends who never crossed paths. But we appreciated our differences. We learned from each other aspects of life that had been completely foreign to both of us only months ago.

I remember telling Vanessa while we were walking to the marriage license office, "I still don't plan to get a job, you know?"

"I have a job. We won't starve," she said.

"I will continue to make weird decisions that nobody understands," I said.

"But I understand. That's all that counts," she replied.

"I will always…"

Before I could finish, Vanessa stopped me. "Listen, I can't cook. I don't do housework. I have a bad temper. I don't have a university degree. I don't like intellectual conversations because they bore me. But you decided those things don't matter. Well, same here. I chose you—*you*, the person, with all your weirdness and eccentricities. I think we are a perfect match because neither one of us demands that the other person change. You are the only person who will accept me for what I am. I am the only person who will take you for who you are and truly appreciate you. Just be yourself. I know I will be myself. I don't know any other way!"

We had met in late April. Six months later, on October 5, 2004, we were married. Tia, now the new station manager at Beijing Radio, was our MC, and Rudy stood next to me with a proud wide grin.

We had no money. I had no job. On Vanessa's meager salary, we lived in her three-hundred-square-foot apartment that was messy and filled to the roof with stuff. I felt I had to clean it up. Every day, I'd sort a pile and ask Vanessa in the evening, "What is this? Can I throw it away? What about this little sticky that has a number on it? Is it important?" This work took a month.

One day I asked her, "How about this old Canadian bank statement? Do you still have an active account there?" She told me no. But just to make sure, I called the bank long distance. As it turned out, it *was* an active account and she still had money in it, only she had totally forgotten. Two weeks later, I found another active account with a significant amount of cash in it. We decided to use this money as down payment to buy a new home.

Vanessa sounded apologetic and a bit embarrassed about her inattention to detail. But I told her, "Don't change. Your easygoing nature helped keep the money available until we were married. My meticulousness helped find the money. This is proof that we are a perfect match!" Vanessa would be precisely the partner I would need by my side as I moved to open China up to the field of psychology.

Growing Panes

One of the Canadian teachers in Vanessa's school was diagnosed with cancer. The teacher had to return to Canada for treatment. Vanessa convinced me to be a substitute teacher until a replacement was found. So, I became an English teacher for English language learners.

On the first day, I opened the class by asking all students to write a letter to the stricken teacher.

"Here are my rules: You can make as many mistakes in grammar and spelling as you wish. It will not cost you points. I don't care how many mistakes you make. This needs to be a letter from the heart that touches the heart. After all, language is a communication tool. The purpose of the letter is to convey what you want the reader to feel. If you write a letter perfect in grammar and spelling but I don't feel anything, it receives an F! But if it makes my eyes red, it is an A! If it makes me cry, it's a 100%!"

As everyone started to write, I noticed a student named Amboise who just sat there. I walked over.

"I noticed you did not write anything."

In Chinese, Amboise explained, "Mr. Yin, do you know how bad my English is? The only reason that I am in this program is because my dad donated a large sum to the school. I can't even say a complete sentence in English, and I have never received anything better than 10 on a scale of 100. There is no way I can write a letter."

"What do you think of the teacher?"

"She is the most wonderful person I know."

"But she has cancer. We don't know if she will live for much longer. We just—we just don't know. Now, how does that make you feel? Do you feel anything? Anything at all?"

"Of course I do!"

"Good! Now, this is your only chance to let her know how you feel. Find a way to communicate to her on this piece of paper. If you can't write a complete sentence, write a partial sentence. If you can't write a partial sentence, write a few isolated words. If you can't write a single word, draw a picture. Just tell yourself, *I have this feeling in my heart that I must find a way to convey to her. If I don't do this, I will live a life with regret. I will find a way to do this—any way!*"

> *If you can't write a partial sentence, write a few isolated words. If you can't write a single word, draw a picture. Just tell yourself,* I have this feeling in my heart that I must find a way to convey to her.

"I will try…" he took a deep breath and tapped his pencil lightly on the desk.

Amboise sat there for ten more minutes, then he picked up his pen. Half an hour later, he handed me his letter. I read it and cried. The letter contained four "words" and the only word spelled correctly was the word "I," which is rather impossible to spell wrong. It said "U sik, I pane!" *You sick, I pain.* Tears rolled down my face. I hugged Amboise.

"I just read the best letter I have ever read in my life. You are a wonderful student, Amboise! More importantly, you are a wonderful human being. Listen, I will only be your teacher for a few weeks. When I leave, a letter like this might only get you 10 points, not 100. But don't mind that. Forget about the grade. Just do everything with your heart and express yourself with courage, without worrying about making mistakes or what other people think of you. Keep up your good work!"

In another incident two weeks later, I was told that the school decided to kick out a troublemaker named Billy. In addition to being another "my dad donated lots of money, therefore, I am in the program" kid, he smoked on campus, drank beer in the dorm, and was disruptive in class. The school had finally decided Billy must go! When I heard this, I walked to the principal's office and asked him to give the kid one more chance.

> *Those boarding schools were like prison camps. They'd beat me. When I made a mistake, they'd stab the back of my hands with a pencil. The backs of my hands looked like a Dalmatian.*

I called Billy to my office. He did not look a bit concerned.

"Billy, I don't particularly care about your grade, which is rather close to zero. But I want to know, why do you have no sense of discipline whatsoever? Is it really that difficult to have even the most minimal amount of self-control?"

Billy showed me the backs of his hands.

"Do you see these black dots? Ever since kindergarten, my parents were so busy making money that they sent me to boarding school. I saw them twice a year. That's all. Those boarding schools were like prison camps. They'd beat me. When I made a mistake, they'd stab the backs of my hands with a pencil. The backs of my hands looked like a Dalmatian.

"Here, I finally am in a school that treats me like a human being. People here are humane. I have tasted freedom for the first time in my life. Whatever I do, there's no beating. It's impossible for me to control myself. I want to taste freedom every second. Do you understand?"

I nodded. "I see your point."

"I don't study because I am just too far behind to even understand a single word in class."

"What kind of life do you want when you grow up, Billy?" I asked.

"You want the truth? My parents are super rich. I will never need to work. My life will be eat, drink, play, talk nonsense, and chase women."

"What a beautiful dream, Billy! I hope your wish can come true!"

Billy looked shocked at my response.

"I want to help you realize your dream, Billy. Eat, drink, play, talk nonsense, and chase women. What a life! However, the way you're going, you aren't going to live that dream."

"Why not?"

"First of all, once you enter adult life, every circle has its rules. Even the jungle has rules of the jungle. If you have no sense of rules, no sense of adapting yourself and making certain considerations to accommodate others, you will be kicked out of every circle you try to join. They may eat, drink, play, talk nonsense, and womanize, but it will be without you as a member of the gang."

Billy looked concerned.

"The other thing is this: Most people learn and grow all their lives. In a few years, talking nonsense will become talking about something. If you have no sense of learning, soon they will be talking about things you know nothing about. They wouldn't want to talk to you anymore."

Now Billy looked really worried.

"I don't care about your grade. Frankly, I don't necessarily agree with all the rules either. But school is the place where one learns about rules, learns to respect rules, and develops a habit of learning that will help him continue to grow and develop even after school. That is why you need school. That is why you need to have basic discipline and participate in learning."

Billy was quiet. Then he said, "But they kicked me out. What now?"

"I have asked the school to give you one last chance. This is how we will do it. You are suspended for a week. You must leave the campus right now. On your way home, I want you to buy at least three newspapers."

"Newspapers? Which ones?"

"Doesn't matter. Any three. When you get home, I want you to read every page, every word, even the ads."

Billy looked puzzled, but he listened attentively.

"Tomorrow, I want you to buy the same three papers again. Since you read everything the first day, on the second day, I want you to concentrate on articles or reports that cover the same topics. For instance, if there is an article on the Middle East on the first day, and there is another article on Iraq, that would be one to follow up on. Or the topic could be migrant workers, inflation, Sino-U.S. relations, whatever."

"And the point of this is?"

"Do this for the entire week. At the end of the week, through learning, you will understand a topic that you previously knew nothing about."

"Oh! That's interesting!" Billy's eyes lit up.

"On Monday, come to my office. I'll prepare tea and biscuits. We'll have a debate on two topics of your choice. If the discussion is to my satisfaction, I will recommend that the school take you back."

"Do you have that power?"

"Yes. And more importantly, you do."

Billy came back the following week a different person. Our discussion on Afghanistan went for two hours, after which I took him to lunch and we continued with the crisis of water resources in Northern China. He did more than I asked. He spent hours each night reading, looking up information on the Internet, and conducting research.

It took five weeks before the replacement teacher arrived. In those weeks, I taught twenty-five classroom hours a week. But I spent more than that amount of time on these students outside of classroom hours. Let me tell you, Amboise and Billy were my two favorite students. I had the feeling that I was sent to this school as a substitute teacher just for them.

> *I had the feeling that I was sent to this school as a substitute teacher just for them.*

A few years later, I met Amboise in Winnipeg. He had been accepted into a university program. Some months after that, I was surprised when I saw Billy at a Starbucks, reading a book on marketing while he sipped his cappuccino.

Many kids like Amboise and Billy were children of China's newly rich who were poorly educated people and seized the first opportunities offered by economic reform. Many of them were so busy making money that they had no time for their children. They "solved the problem" by throwing money at it. Their children became spoiled brats. I'm glad that I was given the opportunity to turn two of these kids around.

One of these days, I thought, *I will need to work on the parents!*

Fame

Just before the New Year, 2005, I noticed a TV program being broadcast from Beijing where a man named Doctor Hong Zhaoguang was giving a lecture to elderly people about physical health. I thought it would be a good idea to see if I could work with him on his lecture circuit to add a mental health component. So, I contacted the Institute. Doctor Hong was famous for his medical expertise, so I wasn't sure if I would get a reply. But, a representative gave me a call and informed me that I was exactly what they were looking for. They offered me the position of executive director. I was amazed at this opportunity!

The Zhaoguang Institute of Public Health had a large roster of health experts. Among them, Dr. Hong was obviously the star draw. With me on board, they now had a mental health expert.

I went on a few lecture tours with Dr. Hong, mostly to get familiarized with the business end of the process. It was more complicated than I thought, with so many intricacies and nuances that I never knew before. No wonder Rudy's plans never worked! On some occasions, we'd split the duties, with Dr. Hong speaking for ninety minutes about physical health, and me speaking for ninety minutes on mental health. Other times we would share the whole session, but I was always with Dr. Hong.

From that day on, I continued giving solo lectures around the country. Crowds were between eight hundred and four thousand.

That is until one day in May of that year when I was asked to do my first solo engagement.

I couldn't wait for it to start. The meeting room was at a senior center and was not particularly large. A few hundred seniors were crammed into it. The local TV and radio stations were there. It was a major event locally Typical of my style, I had no PowerPoint presentation, no outline, no well-prepared lines or segments. It was off-the-cuff stuff, but it went beautifully. Everyone was smiling.

When it was over, I was surrounded by the audience members. They were posing questions and asking if I had time for some private chats. I did my best to accommodate. I was busy in my hotel room until eleven at night. Just before I went to bed, I got a text from my boss: "A Star is Born!"

I started to receive fan mail. A ninety-five-year-old gentleman said no one had touched his heart like that since he was a teen. An eighty-five-year-old woman said she now knew how to get along with her daughter-in-law and grandkids. A school teacher told me her parents were so much more pleasant after they attended the lecture.

From that day on, I continued giving solo lectures around the country. Crowds ranged between eight hundred and four thousand.

Just when everything seemed to be going well, I began to have doubts. One problem had to do with a difference in philosophy between myself and The Institute. The Institute insisted that pricing must be firmly high, and availability must be limited. By limiting availability, if you want to get a star speaker, it is almost like engaging in an auction. I could see how this seemed like a good business model. However, I wanted to engage as many people from all ages and all walks of life as possible. I did not want to limit my availability. My goal was to spread the benefit of good mental health to as many people as we could.

Our other disagreement had more to do with content. The business manager wanted "proven products." In other words, he wanted to have one or two lectures that were well-designed down to the smallest details—almost like a staged play, where every anecdote, every story, almost every line, was written out. This would ensure top quality and effect. My problem with that was that I wanted to reach people from a broad spectrum of society. They would each have different backgrounds, different lifestyles, and, most importantly, different needs. I never knew what I'd talk about until I stood on the stage and *looked* at the audience.

I am not a deliverer of a product. I talk to actual human beings, and I try to help them in areas in which they need help. I deliver it the way I think is best for them to receive the message. We may have built the best platform for delivering health and mental health education in China. The business plan made perfect sense, but it didn't seem to serve my ultimate purpose.

Three months after "a star was born," I resigned just like when I left the State of California and Silicon Valley. I left when things were going swimmingly. I resigned without a replacement plan. I just knew that to continue would be wasting my time and delaying my goal. This path might be adjacent to my path, but it was not my path. It was time to move on.

"I resigned today," I said when I got home.

Vanessa's eyebrows raised ever so slightly.

"The reason I resigned is—"

Vanessa put one index finger on my lips. "No, don't explain. I trust you. I trust your judgment. You know what's best for you. Do what you must. I support you unconditionally." Then she kissed me. "So, what will you do now."

"Meditate and wait," I replied.

"For how long?"

I smiled. "Not very long. I think I am ready. I believe someone or something will be presented my way any minute!"

"Even if it doesn't happen right away, it's all right." She kissed me again.

Big Ideas

But it did happen right away! The very next day, I got a call from Tia.

"Hello, Director Yin! How's everything with the Institute?" she asked.

"I just resigned yesterday. I had a feeling you'd call, only I didn't expect it so soon!" I laughed.

"I'm getting better at this timing thing," she laughed. "But seriously, I have a friend I'd like you to meet. His name is Sasha. He's a director at the TV station. He is doing a TV show and is looking for a psychology expert. I immediately thought of you."

That very evening, I met Sasha at a local country club. He was from Beijing and was a few years younger than I. He had chosen a Russian name because Russian was his major in college. Sasha told me his plan for the TV show. It would be sponsored by Huaxia Psychological Education—an education institution for training psychological counselors. I listened.

"An interesting idea . . ."

"Okay. You're not excited," Sasha guessed. "What do you have in mind?"

"No, I don't have reservations when it comes to the show . . . it's a wonderful idea. I'm sure I can play a role in it, and I probably will agree to do so. But . . ."

"You have better ideas? Tell me! I want to hear! Tia said you're a man of ideas and passion! Let me hear them!" He gave me an encouraging smile.

So, I told him that I wanted to meet people where they were in their mental health journey. A scripted, prescribed, "canned" response to situations was *not* what I would want. I explained that I wanted to open the Chinese culture to the healing powers of the field of psychology. Also, I wanted to break the stigma attached to seeking mental health. "I know this has nothing to do with your TV show. But this is what I want to do, eventually. I am working toward that end."

> *I thought idealists had died out in China. I am so glad to meet you! I used to be an idealist. But practical reality is pulling me back. I love your ideas. I want to help you make them come true! I think we can pull it off!*

Sasha sighed. "Paul, I thought idealists had died out in China. I am so glad to meet you! Because I used to be an idealist, but practical reality has restricted me. I love your ideas. I want to help you make them come true, and I think we just might be able to pull it off!"

"This will require organization, money, people, everything. Over the past year I've learned how complicated this is," I said, dejected.

Sasha smiled. "Well, let's get the government involved! In China, government is the most important resource. Not everyone realizes this, but there is a government organization called Office for the Promotion of Spiritual Civilization. Their role is vaguely defined as overseeing 'things that promote a better civilized society.' Every year, they need to do things within that realm. It's their job. They need to hand in a report to their superiors on what they did in any given year.

"Let me tell you, it's an office made up of wonderful people, and they are always on the lookout for new ideas. Let's draw up a plan based on what you want to do and give it to them. We can then make changes until they can agree on it. After that, we do all the work and give them all the credit. Let it be their project. This way, we can get all the necessary permits, better media cooperation, better rates at the venues we rent, everything!" His eyes were beaming.

"But what about the cost?" I shook my head. I was still not quite at Sasha's level of excitement.

"That's where Huaxia comes in. They wanted to do this TV show to raise mental health awareness, but they have no plan for implementation. When there's greater mental health awareness and greater acceptance of psychological intervention, there will be more people who come to their certification training. It's called 'preparing the market.' We can ask them to sponsor *our* project instead. Your idea is the best I have heard so far in raising mental health awareness and acceptance of psychological intervention."

"But my ideas involve changing the whole mindset of China," I said.

"Trust me, they like huge ideas—well, huge ideas that work. For the government, it looks good politically. For Huaxia, it creates greater visibility. Don't be afraid to be huge. Huge can be good!"

I wasn't holding my breath, but I agreed to be on board. For the next month, Sasha lobbied all the parties. We met every few days to make adjustments.

As I sat at the conference table for one of those meetings, Sasha smiled at me. "I made some changes to our plan. I actually put more in there than you said originally, just to prove that I am an even bigger idealist dreamer, ha! We will start on New Year's Day, which is on a Saturday. For the whole year, we will give one free public lecture every Saturday, *fifty-two Saturdays*, on *fifty-two* different mental health topics." Then he winked. "It's your job to come up with fifty-two different topics."

"*Fifty-two?* Really?" I was incredulous, but I immediately started thinking of the possibilities.

"Yep! So, every Thursday, we will publish our free public lecture topic in three Beijing newspapers." Then he winked, "This is the advantage of having government involvement."

"I see." And I really was starting to see Sasha's vision. A smile spread across my face.

Sasha continued, "Every Saturday, those who have read the topic on Thursday and have decided that it's a topic of interest, can come to our free public lecture. This will go on for the entire year." He paused. "Imagine! Fifty-two different topics! There will be a topic for everyone!"

Now I was smiling so big that a joyful laugh almost escaped my lips. "Sasha, this is even bigger than my original idea. But now you have me thinking … can I add a few more requirements?" I felt like I had just rubbed a magic lamp.

"Okay, shoot!"

I asked Sasha if we could organize free mentoring for any inexperienced counselors who attended the lectures, and I wanted to offer at least one free session to anyone in attendance who wanted counseling.

> *One man is not enough. I want to use this opportunity to train a small army.*

Sasha nodded in approval, but I had one more request.

"Also, at some point, I'd like to try having a partner or a team for some of the lectures, so they will eventually be able to do similar things on their own. One man is not enough. I want to use this opportunity to train a small army."

"I think we can do that." Sasha was busy writing things down.

We agreed that our project would be called Mental Health China. The financial sponsor would be Huaxia, and they would pay all the costs including personnel. I couldn't believe it. What a wonderful way to spend this New Year's Day!

Heaven Kisses Earth

It was New Year's Eve, 2005, just before midnight. The fireworks outside had already started to commemorate the onset of 2006. Sasha and I had completed all the preparations for the lectures which were slated to begin on New Years' Day. I went to bed and I slept well. When I awoke, I saw Vanessa, already up and dressed, sitting at the vanity. She was looking at me in the reflection as she pulled a comb briskly through her hair.

"How did you sleep so well on a night like this, just before your big event? I was too nervous to sleep. I guess I'm the only person who truly understands how important today is to you. You have been working toward this day for half your life." She came over to sit beside me.

"Yes, that's true. For much of that time, I had no idea whether this day would ever come."

"If I were you, I wouldn't be able to sleep. You know, I stayed up all night. Aren't you nervous at all?"

I reached for her hand and rubbed it lightly. "A few days ago, I thought I might be nervous today. But I am as calm as I've ever been. Do you know why? It's because I think heaven, earth, and humanity are perfectly aligned. Everything is in place. All I need to do is to do what I know—no more, no less. And I am ready. Are you planning to attend the lecture?"

"No, I can't. I'm too nervous. I might even make you nervous with my presence! I'll be home chilling the champagne."

The first lecture was to be at a lecture hall at Capital Normal University. I arrived a half hour before the lecture was to start. This was New Year's Day, not a day when people normally attended a lecture, but at thirty minutes before the start time the place was already filled to capacity. Just minutes before the start, more people came and had to stand in the square outside the building. Although it was winter, close to a hundred people stood outside in the cold, determined to listen to this lecture.

Sasha needed to delay the start by fifteen minutes as they worked to get two large speakers and a monitor hooked up outside the building. Once that was done, the stage was mine. I have never been so relaxed and confident as I grabbed the microphone and started my lecture: "Good Mental Health is the Key to a Long, Happy Life."

The lecture was supposed to be seventy-five minutes, but I continued for almost two hours. It was like sharing joy with best friends. The atmosphere in the

> *A better world starts with you. Today is only the beginning.*

lecture hall was one of peace and love. At the end, I said, "By making yourself a mentally healthy individual, you are contributing to a happy family. By making your family a happy family, you are contributing to building a better world. A better world starts with you. Today is only the beginning. Please join me on this journey together! Thank you!"

I heard the gentle notes of Schumann's *Mondnacht* start playing in my head; I felt like every note was composed just for me in that moment. It was indeed as if heaven had kissed the earth, and the earth now must dream of heaven. When I stood center stage to a standing ovation, my eyes filled with tears. They were tears of joy and gratitude. I was in heaven!

The Golden Team

Two thousand six had started with a bang. It all happened so fast and so perfectly. I immediately thought of Rudy. I tried to give him a call to tell him about my success and that I was now contracted for fifty-two lectures! But most importantly, I wanted to tell him, "Brother, I wouldn't be here without you. You helped lay the foundation. No one can see the foundation since it is not visible. But I know, and I owe you my gratitude." Unfortunately, I have never had the opportunity to say those words to Rudy. Life seems to have swallowed Rudy up and I've been unable to locate him.

Maybe Rudy's plans never exactly worked out, but I knew for sure that without his energy and enthusiasm I would never have made it to this point.

I often hear people say, "Oh, I wish I had not made all those mistakes and all those wrong turns earlier." But that's wrong. There were no wrong turns. They were all necessary turns, without which this "right turn" would never have happened.

Back home, Vanessa was waiting with the champagne.

"Vanessa, you seem even happier than I am," I said.

"Happy? Yes, of course, but I think more relieved than happy! I was so worried about today. I was afraid something might go wrong."

"Nothing can go wrong today. Heaven, earth, and humanity are aligned. The universe is in a conspiracy to make this happen perfectly." I smiled.

"And you are really going to do it for fifty-two weeks? Fifty-two different topics? Do you have fifty-two different topics now?" She furrowed her eyebrows.

"No, not yet. We will think of them as we go. Doing fifty-two different topics can be a big challenge, but we will do it."

"Why do you always have to do it the hard way? Why all fifty-two weeks? Without a single break? If I were you, my head would explode!" She made the *kaboom* sound and opened her fingers wide in front of her face.

"Vanessa, do you remember the scene in *Good Will Hunting*, where Sean said to Will:

'It's not your fault.
It's not your fault.
It's not your fault.
It's not your fault.
It's not your fault'?"

"How could I forget?" said Vanessa. "It's the most memorable scene in that movie."

"What do you think would have happened if he had just said 'It's not your fault' on time? Or twice? It wouldn't have had much effect, right? At first, people might talk themselves out of coming. But eventually one of the topics has to hit a nerve. I will try to cover every situation one can think of.

> *The goal is that people will begin to understand mental health and its benefits! It will no longer be taboo to say, 'I need help! I can't do this alone!'*

"The goal is that people will begin to understand mental health and its benefits! We will lay the foundation for change. It will no longer be taboo to say, 'I need help! I can't do this alone!' We need to mindfully and deliberately lay this groundwork.

"Removing that stigma won't come from only a few lectures. This comes from a relentless, sustained pounding of the message into their heads. You know me. I don't take shortcuts. I will be persistent and unrelenting." As I looked at her, I felt my confidence rise just in sharing the plan!

"Sounds almost like chasing a girl." She giggled and threw me an accusatory look.

I laughed. "I wasn't that unrelenting, was I?"

Sasha had indeed gathered the small "army" I had asked for. He sent me Gem Yan and Lily Zhang. Gem was a young, incredibly talented, and knowledgeable psychologist with whom I clicked right away. She had a kind, warm personality and a sparkle in her eye. One could not help but be drawn to her. Lily was a very competent psychologist. Her hair was cut with bangs that ran bluntly across her forehead and collided with her small round spectacles. Lily was extremely efficient and paid close attention to administrative details. She kept our little team grounded.

And, as it turned out, one of the best things I took away from my time spent on these fifty-two lectures was that important connection with Gem and Lily. We ended up being referred to as "The Golden Team." We joined together for several lectures and, to me, we were indeed a golden team. Little did the three of us know, we would meet again in the future to provide support for an especially critical event in Beijing's history.

Chapter 7

FINDING TRUE NORTH

The compass needle points home,
But the binocular has no peripheral vision.
~Paul Yin, "Distance"

Psychology *Finally* Does Have a Place in China

After working with the Mental Health China project and giving the fifty-two free public lectures, I began to see evidence of increased public awareness of the importance of mental health and psychological well-being. I had become a recognized celebrity of sorts, with TV appearances, radio shows, magazine columns, and offers coming from a variety of sources including teaching opportunities and business partnerships. Now was the time to take this momentum and push forward.

But I immediately realized that "push" was not the right word. If I pushed according to my will and judgment, I might just get back into the mode of fighting against the current, even though the current was friendlier than before. Or, I might become successful at something that would become too good to let go, leading to a successful life but not one that I wanted. Instead, the wiser thing to do was to take one step back and get a broader view and be patient. It's nice to have goals, but too much focus on personal goals can be a dangerous thing.

I wanted to take a rest and write a book or two. The first book was about personal mental health and was entitled *A Good Mental Outlook=A Good Life*. It was finished in about a month and was published. As it turned out, the rest and the writing were interrupted unexpectedly. Several things happened that caused my path to veer in a different direction for the next several years.

The Mental Health China project had not just been a personal success for me. It had been a business success for Huaxia as well. With the high number of people signing up for training, they decided to embark on a companion project. They decided they wanted to establish the Employee Assistance Program (EAP) in China. This program was widely available in most western countries as a way for people to obtain access to mental health care through their place of employment for both personal and work-related issues. They asked me to assist in making this happen.

I was ecstatic. This was exactly what needed to happen to begin removing the stigma attached to mental health assistance in China. Now people would have easier access to trained counselors and the support that they needed.

One of the stumbling blocks in bringing the EAP to China, however, was that most mental health professionals there had limited business experience, so they had no idea how to apply it in a business setting.

There was also the problem of cultural differences that China presented. I agreed that I could make a difference. But I knew that even with increased awareness and acceptance, it would still be a long time before individuals would recognize their own need for intervention and seek help in a professional setting.

I realized that the corporate and organizational setting was the perfect platform to start increasing mental health awareness and apply it in real life settings. Because people would be more comfortable as members of an organization and dealing with the problems within the organization, it would still be considered "in-house and within the walls." That would generate far less stigma than going outside for help.

Besides, when the leaders of organizations truly realized that not addressing the problems would be costing the organization productivity, the boss would be highly motivated to make sure that the organization prioritized health. Unlike political leaders, who sometimes may go for a flashy show, business leaders were looking for concrete results.

With John Maynard and Brenda Blair, I trained the first group of EAP professionals in China. This annual training continued for five years.

> *With John Maynard and Brenda Blair, I trained the first group of EAP professionals in China.*

Through those years, I also mentored many of those students as they initiated their own EAP programs. Many of them asked me to become a partner in their new businesses. But I had decided against this. I did not invest a single penny or accept a large annual salary. My goal was to help EAP to develop and prosper in China. I wanted every one of my students to have a chance to succeed. Had I joined up with any one of the students, it would have put the other students at a disadvantage. I'd be competing with my own students. That would not have been fair, and it would not be good for developing the EAP in China.

It was at one of these EAP training sessions that I first met Caesar who would become such an important part of my future. I was told that I would have a new co-trainer to work with.

I was in a hotel conference room with a few other counselors when suddenly someone flung open the door. In burst a Chinese man, younger than I, with slick black hair, and movie-star good looks. He was in mid-conversation with a small group of people behind him. Everyone in the room paused to watch his progression into the room. He wore trousers with suspenders, and his sleeves were rolled up to his elbows. An expensive watch glistened at his wrist.

"All right," he said, turning to address our group. "What's the plan here? Are we going to make this happen or what?"

"This is Mr. Yin," one of the assistants told him.

Caesar was taken aback. "Oh! I have heard so much about you, sir. It is such a privilege to be able to work with you. I look forward to learning from this experience." The pompous air was gone from his tone and he reached out to shake my hand vigorously.

Caesar and I split the training sessions between the two of us. At the final combined session, I gave a short speech.

"Ladies and gentlemen, when I was in college, it took me a long time to decide on my major. After college, it took me a long time to settle on a career path. But I was not a disillusioned youth. I had a clear vision. I said to myself, 'Even though I do not know yet what I want to do, I want it to enable me to say when I am lying on my deathbed and looking back at my life: this world is a better place because I was here.'

"We've all been idealists at one point or another in our lives. We want to become an important person in history—a person who makes major contributions to humanity. But then reality hits. Too many of us live such busy lives that we can't find meaning in our work.

"However, I am so happy for you today. Today you will start a journey with EAP which will make workplaces better for everyone. It will make thousands, then tens of thousands, of families happier and their lives brighter. It will enable you to say, 'This world is now a better place because I was here.' Isn't this exciting?

"I want you to look at the people around you. Many of those people will become your future competitors. That does not make you enemies. We are all partners in the same cause. If you lose a contract to one of your classmates, congratulate him. If you hear someone else had her contract renewed, celebrate with her. We should rejoice because it means that thousands of families will have the help and assistance that they need. Rejoice also because her success means that more companies will want to invest in EAP. Your future customers will come from her success. Everyone's victory is *our* victory!

"Let's pull for each other and help each other. Let's work together to help EAP grow in China!"

For the next several years, Caesar was a frequent partner in these trainings. During the breaks and sometimes right in the middle of a private conversation, he had this habit of excusing himself to go into a corner to make or take

> *Your future customers will come from her success. Everyone's victory is our victory!*

an important call. Even from a distance, you could tell from his body language during some of these calls that he had morphed into a completely different persona.

People were really drawn to Caesar's charisma, but at the same time, there were people who couldn't stand him. A couple of people quietly whispered words of warning into my ears about him. It wasn't hard for me to see some of his obvious flaws. Here was a hard-driven young man full of ambition who would say anything, do anything, and wear any mask that was necessary to achieve his personal goals. Meanwhile, I wasn't even sure if he knew who he was, or maybe he knew but didn't want to acknowledge. Maybe he was running away from something. He was racing a hundred miles an hour toward goals that may ultimately destroy him.

Vaguely, I saw something in Caesar that reminded me of a younger me. Instead of heeding the warnings of some well-meaning friends, I decided I wanted to help, maybe even to save, this young man.

EAP Gets an African Connection

The gradual growth and success of EAP in China did not go unnoticed. I gave a presentation about the effect of cultural differences in EAP that generated a lot of interest. It gained the attention of the broader Employee Assistance Professionals Association (EAPA) conference.

Because of that attention, I was invited to Nigeria to be involved in a training, again conducted by Brenda Blair. From there I was invited to be the international keynote speaker in Cape Town by Tshif, the president of the South Africa EAPA. I had met Tshif two years before at my first international conference. We were like kindred spirits. He told me that his dream was to have EAP available in all of Africa. The growth of EAP had been difficult. But since he had heard some of my ideas and innovations, he thought that they might prove helpful.

"We have no money," he said. "You will have to pay for your own trip here."

"I'm not in it for the money," I said. "I'm in it for exciting opportunities like this! Let's make a difference!"

Cape Town quickly became one of my favorite cities in the world. This was my first visit, but somehow it already felt like home. Part of that was because of the tremendous welcome from my friend, Tshif.

When I got on the stage for my keynote speech, I started by saying "*Ni hao!*"

"*Ni hao* is how we greet each other in China. I know we have almost twenty languages in this conference hall. Now, please, greet the people around you in your native language."

The room suddenly became animated. Then I said "*Ni hao*," again. "What do you think *Ni hao* means? No, *Ni hao* does not mean 'how are you.' *Ni hao* actually means 'you are fine.' That's right. In China, we don't greet people by asking them 'how are you?' Let's face it, most of the time you don't really want to know. You are not asking a question, and you aren't really interested in an answer. You don't want to hear 'I've had a lousy day' or 'could be better.' In China, we don't even give you a chance to be anything but fine.

"Now, let's greet each other the Chinese way. Turn to the person next to you and say, 'You are fine!'"

I walked to the podium and scanned the audience.

"You are probably thinking, 'EAP is essentially a western concept. So, why is the international keynote speaker from China?' What do you expect a keynote speaker from China to talk about?"

The African audience was exceptionally interactive! People started shouting their responses:

"Table tennis!"

"Martial arts!"

"Kung Fu!"

"Yes, Kung Fu!"

"Aha!" I put on a Kung Fu stance. "So, I will start by talking about Kung Fu. There are many schools of Kung Fu that you may have heard about. Which school of Chinese Martial Arts is generally considered the most powerful?"

"Shaolin!"

"Wutang!"

"Tai Chi!"

"Yes, I think it is Tai Chi!"

"Tai Chi!"

"Right! Tai Chi is generally considered the most powerful one. How many people here know Tai Chi?" I asked.

> *Every energy and every available force in the universe is my friend.*

After seeing only a few isolated raised hands, I said, "Since most of you don't seem to know Tai Chi, let me do a demonstration."

I moved a few feet away from the podium. I took a series of deep breaths and closed my eyes. I slowly, deliberately moved my arms and legs in several fluid postures without pausing between. When I finished, I stepped back to the podium.

"Many of you must be wondering, 'How can this slow, sleepy, meditative exercise be considered the most powerful martial art? How is this possible?'"

Now I had them interested.

"Tai Chi is the most powerful because behind Tai Chi is a philosophy which says, 'I am not fighting against anything. Every energy and every available force in the universe is my friend. I will use the energy that is available in the universe to serve a positive purpose.'

"In your country and in mine, those of us in the mental health profession have many enemies. There is the ignorance of the general public. There are some politicians who only want their own political gain. There are businessmen who only care about profit. There are centuries-old traditions that no longer make sense. Every day we fight against them. But instead of fighting against so many enemies, why not adopt the Tai Chi philosophy?

"If you feel you must make the company, society, and family into something more like an American company and society, you are destined to fail. Your society is and will always be African. You are an African first and a mental health professional second.

"Ask yourself, 'How can I use the negative forces to work *for me* to make this a better world?'"

Between learning African dances and taking yoga lessons, I talked with many people about specific programs. But most of all, I talked with my kindred spirit friend, Tshif, about his dream of a Pan African Conference and spreading EAP throughout the African continent. We talked about specific countries like Ghana, Kenya, Tanzania, and Swaziland.

The following year, Tshif and the South Africa Branch received an international award at the EAPA conference. It was an important moment for him, for Africa, and for EAP.

A Turning Point

I received a call from a representative for one of the offices of the Chinese Psychological Association asking me if I'd like to be on the board of directors.

"Why me?" I asked. "I come with no official titles of any kind."

"One of the esteemed members of the board passed away. We have an opening that needs to be filled. You have done so much in promoting good mental health that many people recommended you for the board. We thought it would be a refreshing change to have someone on the board who isn't from within the system," she said.

"Aren't there lots of other people who would like to be on the board of directors?" I asked.

"Of course! Who wouldn't want to have that position?" she said. "In this field, it is probably the most valuable title there is. Everyone would love to have it."

"In that case, let someone else have it," I said. "I have no use for it. Why should I take it away from someone for whom it might be useful and valuable? I have always been on the outside. I have never had an official title of any kind. I don't need one. But for someone who is working within the system, this title is a very big deal."

"But Mr. Yin," she interrupted me. "I'm sure by having the title you will be able to do your current work even more effectively."

She sounded right. But I continued, "Not exactly. By being outside of the system and having no titles, I have no conflict of interest with anyone. I am not a threat to anyone. This makes me a potential partner with anyone on any project. I am and will always be a free spirit. I like it this way." I thanked her kindly, but turned down the offer.

"So, what they tell me about you is true." She laughed. "I guess you're right. If you take this position, more people will be convinced that you must have other agendas and that you are just waiting for the bigger fish."

As far as I was concerned, my job was done. EAP had gone from a brand-new concept into a fast-growing new field. It was now in very good, competent hands. I wished them well.

To many people, it seemed that that was the day that I left EAP. But I knew I'd never truly leave. My love for humanity and service is too strong. It has become a way of being. Whenever I am needed, I will be there. Otherwise, it was time for me to move on and leave my footprints on another swath of sand.

Chapter 8

THE EARTH QUAKES

Every year, we all have our struggles as well as our joys. They are all divine gifts. Making your life meaningful, fulfilling, and beautiful is the best way to prove your worthiness for these gifts. Let's all embrace life and all its riches.
~Paul Yin, "Newsletter"

A Messed up String of Codes

On New Year's Day in 2007, Vanessa and I had met little Louisa for the first time. She was the infant daughter of Sasha and his wife Isolde. His wife began trying to talk us into having a child. This had always been a difficult topic of discussion for Vanessa and me.

Before we got married, Vanessa made it very clear that she did not want to have children. But even though I had no plans for getting married before I met Vanessa, I had always wanted to be a father. Since I loved Vanessa, and she did not want to have babies, I told her I would be okay with that. "But you know, you may change your mind one day!"

Isolde's prodding seemed to have no effect on Vanessa until one day when she said, "You need to do it for Paul! Look how wonderful he is with our daughter! Paul not being a father would be a crime against humanity! The criminal would be you!"

Vanessa agreed, but still said no. However, she did decide to go to the doctor to check on her reproductive health, just to know how many years she might have left to change her mind. The results showed that she would not be able to have babies. She was not fertile.

People can be funny in that circumstance. Vanessa had never wanted to have babies. That was her decision. But when suddenly someone told her that she *couldn't* have babies, she got mad! "What do you mean I can't!" Suddenly, Vanessa wanted to become a mother and she wanted it *now!*

Vanessa told Isolde the test results. Isolde smiled, "I have the perfect solution for you. One of my friends is the best in vitro fertilization specialist in the country. I will connect you with her; she can work miracles!"

Isolde's friend, Dr. Shang, ordered lots of tests for us. When all the results came in, she told us that Vanessa's reproductive system truly was not very good. She said that if we wanted to be successful with in vitro, it would involve at least one, possibly two, operations. Vanessa would then need daily injections for several months.

Unfortunately, Dr. Shang also informed us that, after all those steps, the chance of success was probably less than ten percent. Normally, she would never take on a case involving such a low probability of success, but since we were friends, she would be willing to do her best. She reminded us to proceed thoughtfully and cautiously. The three of us knew how psychologically devastating it may be if we were to put all our hope into something that ultimately failed. And the chances were high that this endeavor would fail.

At home, Vanessa and I just looked at each other. We were afraid to discuss it lest the first person to verbalize his or her thoughts would cement a decision. In a calm and measured tone, I finally said, "Listen. It is clear that if we don't at least give it a try, we may regret it for the rest of our lives; so I think we should give it a try. If it doesn't work, and it's just you and me, it's still perfect."

Vanessa had to give herself shots every day. She gained a lot of weight. But she was determined to make it work. Soon, Dr. Shang said we were ready for the first try. The wait was long and stressful. When the results did come, we learned that we were unsuccessful. Vanessa and I mindfully considered our options and agreed to give it one final try. If this attempt did not work, we were prepared to go into our golden years by ourselves.

On the night before we were to receive the results of our decidedly final attempt to find out if Vanessa could get pregnant, we couldn't sleep. We stayed up all night watching our favorite driver, Kimi Raikkonen, race in the Brazil Grand Prix, the final Formula One race of the season. Kimi was by no means expected to win.

He had been seventeen points behind Hamilton, the frontrunner, with two races to go. The crowning of Hamilton as the Formula One champion seemed to be only a matter of time and formality. But, despite all odds, Kimi won the first race, as Hamilton somehow stalled his car in the gravel and didn't finish. Then, incredibly, he won the final race while Hamilton came in seventh. Kimi got the crown, coming in one point ahead of Hamilton! Vanessa and I were ecstatic!

I suddenly said to Vanessa, "This morning, if we find out that you're pregnant and we are having the baby, let's name the baby Kimi. Kimi Raikkonen winning today is a miracle. It would take a miracle for us to have a baby. Kimi is a good name for either a boy or a girl. What do you think?"

Vanessa smiled. "Kimi is a good name. You know what? I think Kimi winning today was a good omen for us! It means today is a day for miracles to happen! We are going to have a baby!"

When we got to the hospital, Vanessa was too nervous to go inside. "I'll just sit in the car and pray," she said.

"Prayers are good. But remember, whatever the outcome is, I love you. And whatever the outcome is, we have a perfect family." I kissed her and went into the lab.

I waited a half hour. They finally gave me the results. I casually walked out of the building and saw Vanessa in the distance, sitting in the car. I paused. She saw me and held her breath. Suddenly, I gave an enthusiastic fist pump. "Yes!"

Vanessa leaped from the car and we hurried over to Dr. Shang's office. She was ecstatic for us. "You should be happy. This is a miracle. I calculated your chances as three percent. But you did it!" Then she poured a bit of cold water on our joy. "Unfortunately, you're less than half way there. Vanessa, your system is so fragile, we don't know if you can support the baby in your womb for nine months. It's like a seed has been planted and a sprout has been spotted, but the soil is so barren that there is no guarantee that the plant will bear fruit."

> *It's like a seed has been planted and a sprout has been spotted, but the soil is so barren that there is no guarantee that the plant will bear fruit.*

A few months later, Vanessa went to the hospital for an aspiration biopsy and DNA test to see if the embryo was okay. The result was shocking. They found a section of her DNA that was not normal, or, to be more precise, unidentifiable. It was like a section of random codes that was different from normal people. The doctors didn't know what it was. That was alarming. The recommendation was that we terminate the pregnancy, since the baby was obviously not normal. But Vanessa and I weren't ready to just give up at this point after everything we had been through.

"Doctor, you only said the baby's DNA is different from all normal people, but you didn't say that there's definitely something *wrong*," Vanessa said.

"Right, but if genetically you have such a large section of the DNA that is different from everyone else, chances are almost one hundred percent that there's something very wrong, even if we don't know what it is. If we wait for the baby to develop and be born to find out, it might be tragic," the doctor explained.

"But doctor," I cut in. "Even if there is a one percent chance that the baby is all right, we don't want to end his or her chance for life. Is there anything else we could do? Isn't there some other way to clarify this a little more?" I begged.

The doctor thought for a while. "Well, there is. You two can both get your DNA tested. If either one of you has that same section of DNA that is exactly the same as that of your baby, then, since you both seem normal with no obvious health problems, then it means that the section of messed up codes, whatever it is, apparently is harmless. That's the only thing we can try, but we have to rush or it will be too late to terminate the pregnancy."

Vanessa and I both had our DNA tested. We had to wait almost two weeks for the results. The wait was agonizing. Every day, I'd hear Vanessa talk to Kimi saying things like, "Dear Kimi, Mommy loves you. I don't care what the test says. I am having you. I will hold you in my arms. I will kiss you. I will nurse you. I want you to see this world and feel the love from Mommy and Daddy. I don't care what the test says. I really don't! We are having you!"

Two weeks later, we went to get the results of the DNA test. As we walked toward the doctor's office, we were both silent. When we settled in, the doctor handed the results to Vanessa.

He smiled as he told us, "The baby's section of messy codes is exactly the same as that same section from the father's DNA. Since the father appears to be healthy, that means the baby should be all right. You can finally rest easy."

"Oh!" Vanessa let out a scream. She put her hands on her heart to calm its racing. "But . . . is it still a messed up string of codes?"

The doctor smiled. "Well, we don't know what it is. It is different from anyone else. All I can say is, the father must be someone dissimilar to all other people. Whatever it is that makes him weird, your child has apparently picked that up. He or she will be very much like the father."

"Oh, that would be nice!" Vanessa beamed. "I want Kimi to be like him. He is one of a kind. Our Kimi will be one of a kind as well!"

The Joy of Stinky Feet

On May 8th, 2008, when Vanessa was seven months pregnant, she woke up in the early hours from a terrifying nightmare, hysterical and sweating profusely. "Kimi just talked to me in my dream! She said she couldn't breathe! She told me to go the hospital right now and save her!" We both sprang into action. As we hurried to the door, I thought I would pour her a glass of milk since I was worried she would get hungry, but Vanessa insisted that we needed to rush directly to the hospital.

At the doctor's office, Vanessa was quickly hooked up to some monitoring devices. The doctor ordered immediate surgery. "The baby's in trouble. We'll have to take her out as soon as possible!" Then, the doctor asked if Vanessa had an empty stomach. If she did, the surgery could be performed immediately. If not, the doctor said he would wait until the afternoon. Fortunately, she had not had the milk.

> *Kimi just talked to me in my dream! She said she couldn't breathe!*

When Kimi did come out, alive and weighing barely three pounds, the doctors found that her cord had fallen off. Had we not come to the hospital immediately after Vanessa was awakened by her dream, or had Vanessa had that glass of milk, Kimi might not have survived. This tiny little baby had saved her own life!

I was given the task of pushing the little incubator cart from surgery to the ICU. I looked down at this little miracle baby. She was tiny, with a huge head compared to her minute body. She looked purple and almost transparent, like blueberry Jell-O. I was told to go fast, but I was afraid that with every little bump she could fall apart.

As I pushed the cart, Kimi opened her eyes wide, lifted her tiny little hand to move the sheet that partially covered her face, and began to look around. Her eyes were big, bright, and focused, as if eager to see this new world with the life that she herself had made possible.

Kimi was in the ICU for thirty-five days. No less than a dozen times, she was in danger of losing her delicate grip on life. She stopped breathing twice. She needed transfusions, and the hospital was unable to find matching blood. She couldn't drink milk at all for almost three weeks. Her tummy was bloated and hard as rock. Despite that, she bravely fought on.

Every day, my job was to go to the hospital at nine in the morning to get an update of her status and deliver her mother's milk. Kimi's digestive system was not well developed. She couldn't actually drink the milk. The doctor would try a few drops every day. When her stomach turned to hardened stone, they'd suck it out through her nose. They had to keep doing this daily until she could handle the milk. Vanessa gave me several ounces of milk every day to deliver to the hospital. We actually needed less than a teaspoon. "She must be getting bigger," Vanessa said.

"To be sure. There's nothing like mother's milk!" I'd reply. Then I was off to the hospital. Only the medical staff were allowed in with Kimi, but every day I walked back and forth just outside her ward. I'd often stop at the window and talk to her.

"Kimi, I know it is hard right now. But if you can just push through this, do you know what wonders lie ahead? Life is such a beautiful thing. You don't want to miss it. Your Mom and I have so much love for you. We need you to fight through this, so we can show you.

"I have great plans for you. I want you to see the world. I want you to experience everything life has to offer. But my plans don't matter. God will decide if you stay. But you need to show God your will to live. I know you can do it.

"You gave yourself a chance by giving your Mommy that dream. Now, do the rest and fight on! I'm here with you. Together, we can do it! I love you!"

More than a month after Kimi was born, she finally came home. We finally got to hold our Kimi. She weighed even less than her birth weight which was not even three pounds. Her feet were the same size as triple-A batteries, and her ears were like thin sheets of wax paper. Her mouth was so small that the nipple couldn't fit into her mouth. We were afraid we would break her just by holding her.

We had high hopes that we were in the clear, but later that summer, when she was about three months old, Kimi was diagnosed with pneumonia. She had to be admitted and undergo a variety of tests over the course of five days. By the fifth day, the doctor told us she only had a fifty percent chance of making it through the night. "But if she does," he said, "I think she will come out of this unscathed."

Vanessa had already spent four sleepless nights sitting with her at the hospital. With heavy hearts, we agreed that she should go home and try to rest. I would stay by Kimi's bedside.

During the night, Kimi's condition deteriorated from serious to critical. That one night by her side felt like a thousand. The doctors, Kimi, and I fought every second. Kimi's breathing rate was sometimes as low as six breaths per minute. Her heart rate was often over two hundred beats per minute. But

> *During the night Kimi's condition deteriorated from serious to critical.*

oh—how she fought on! I was fighting by her side the whole time, giving her sponge baths to control her temperature and checking the monitors all the time. I worked side by side with the doctor and nurses.

At about four in the morning, Kimi fell asleep. Her breathing had stabilized. Then just before sunrise, Kimi suddenly opened her eyes and lifted one of her feet. That had been one of our father-daughter games. I smiled at her, sniffed her foot, and said, "Stinky little foot!" She smiled back. Although she was exhausted, she told me in her own special way that she had indeed pulled through. I ran outside. Rain started to pour down. I stood in the rain and wept uncontrollably.

Sichuan Earthquake

Kimi was born on May 8, 2008. It was a time of great joy for Vanessa and me. Unfortunately, four days after her birth, a major tragedy befell China. One of the most devastating earthquakes in history hit the Sichuan Province in China. At the Beijing Union Hospital, doctors were being organized to go to the earthquake-affected region. A fund-raising campaign was started. I immediately decided to donate some money in Kimi's name. I attached a letter in her name:

Hello, big brothers and big sisters in Sichuan: My name is Kimi, and I am four days old. Right now, I'm in the Intensive Care Unit at the Beijing Union Hospital fighting for my life. I'm lucky because I'm in the best hospital in China with the best doctors and the most caring nurses helping me. I also have my family firmly behind me.

But I heard that there are other kids not as lucky. There was an earthquake where you are. You may have lost loved ones. You may have lost your home. Some of you are badly injured. As desperate as it may seem at the moment, we can always have the faith to fight and restart our lives so that we can all grow up to be the pillars of our communities. My situation may seem dire, but you need help more than I do. I have asked my parents to donate some of the money they had put aside for my toys and things. Even as kids, we need to pull together because we are not separate individuals. We have a common soul.

I have complete faith that I will eventually pull through. I am sure that you will, too. Maybe we will meet one day. But even if we don't, let's be brothers and sisters who will work together to spread love and make this world a better place for all.

Love, Kimi

With Kimi in the ICU, the most difficult thing every day was to sit in the waiting room and pass the time. Other than signing waivers several times a day as doctors sought to overcome one crisis after another, there was absolutely nothing I could do. I decided that the most productive way to help Kimi was to help others.

In the earthquake regions, communication was effectively broken off. The Red Cross gave radios to people in tents and even air-dropped radios and batteries to villages cut off from the rest of the world. The Central Radio Station started a twenty-four-hour special broadcast to the region.

I decided to join the broadcast team. Every day, I went to the radio station to talk about grief, trauma, PTSD, and other important information that would help them deal with their situation and slowly start a recovery process.

> *Every day, I went to the radio station to talk about grief, trauma, PTSD, and other important information that would help them deal with their situation and slowly start a recovery process.*

A couple days later, some from the first group of journalists who went to cover the earthquake came back. I received a request to help these journalists deal with PTSD. Many people didn't realize how difficult it would be to cover a major disaster like this.

There was one journalist whose main job was to look through thousands of photos to pick the ones to be used in print, TV, and online news. Hours of exposure to some of the most gruesome images had a devastating effect on her.

Another young journalist worked for almost forty-eight hours straight. Then, in the middle of the night, she was taken to a van parked in a vacant lot to rest. When she woke up before sunrise, she was in the middle of a lot filled with corpses. It was surreal.

Upon returning to Beijing, many of these reporters had nightmares, flashbacks, and a variety of physical and emotional symptoms. I held several group sessions for them. Then I decided it would be a good idea to help prep people before going to the front line so they'd be better prepared psychologically and have a better capacity to cope. I started with journalists. Then I helped train counselors, social workers, and medical doctors.

> *There may be plenty of pomp and circumstance on the road with the largest peloton, but it is on the road less traveled that one leaves discernable footprints in the sand.*

Some people may wonder why I didn't go directly to Sichuan to help like many people did. Aside from the fact that I wanted to be with Kimi, it was in fact a conscious decision. With tens of millions of people affected by the earthquake, my being there wouldn't have made much difference. But if I could train over a thousand professional doctors and counselors going to the region, it would have a much bigger impact.

I knew that a major disaster like this would awaken compassion in people, but I also suspected that it wouldn't last. Soon people would go back to their daily lives. PTSD, however, is something that requires long-term care. I would be needed when those with PTSD symptoms would attempt to assimilate back into their everyday lives, since these emergency support systems would have vanished by then.

There may be plenty of pomp and circumstance on the road with the largest *peloton*, but it is on the road less traveled that one leaves discernable footprints in the sand.

I was contacted by Huaxia and asked to work at a center they had opened in the middle of the earthquake's affected area. The program, originally designed for the United Nations (UN) and the World Health Organization (WHO), was to be used in areas with a widespread need for psychological help but with minimal professional personnel available. The ideal trainees were those who had the trust of the people who needed help and who had regular contacts with them.

We immediately thought of training the school teachers who would have immediate and prolonged access to any children, and possibly families, who were affected. Training teachers suited the goal we wanted to achieve.

Before I departed for Sichuan, I got a call from a man whose daughter I had counseled. "Mr. Yin, do you think Serena is ready to go back to school?"

Serena was a Chinese student studying in an American university. During her freshman year, she started to suffer from major depression. It was so bad that her parents both flew to the U.S. to see her. Desperate and not knowing what to do, they called me. After a brief conversation over the phone, I had recommended that she take a year off from school and come back to China for treatment. We had a few sessions and she began to show some improvement, but she was nowhere close to being able to go back to school and live on her own.

"What do *you* think?" I asked her dad.

"Well, to be honest," Serena's dad hesitated, "she's a bit better, but I'm really not sure if she's ready. However, we don't want her to waste too much more time. Her classmates from high school are now a year ahead of her. I think she'd feel ashamed."

I suddenly had an idea.

"Does Serena have some time? I'm about to do some important work, and I would like her to be my assistant."

"Your assistant? Does she qualify? She's just a freshman in college."

"Yes, she's perfectly qualified. In fact, I think it would do tons of good for her recovery," I assured him.

The next morning, Serena arrived in Beijing. Together we flew to Sichuan. She was excited but nervous.

"This is extremely important work," she said. "I am worried that I may screw up. I've never done this before."

"The work you do will be very simple: sorting papers, handing out materials, and the like. But I want you to pay attention in class as if you were a student in training. I want you to do all the exercises just like everyone else. I want you to observe, listen, get to know some people, absorb, think, and reflect. You will learn more here than you will ever learn in college."

"What will I learn?" she asked me.

"That's for you to find out," I replied.

The teachers for the training were selected from local schools. Many of them had lost loved ones in the earthquake. A few of the students were orphaned. Some of the students and many of the parents were feeling suicidal. There was much work to be done.

In between trainings, a small group of us drove to the adjacent town of Hanwang where most of the population had been wiped out in an instant. We saw that the clock on the bell tower was stuck at 2:28, which was the exact time the earthquake hit. The clock tower overlooked the rubble of several completely collapsed buildings. Two signs were still clearly visible: Hanwang Kindergarten and Hanwang Elementary School.

The entire area was cordoned off for safety and to prevent the spread of disease. There was a strong smell of chemicals in the air, and white powdery lime covered the rubble like fresh-fallen snow. At a corner over the rubble, we noticed a tattered, lone teddy bear. It was painful to see the devastation firsthand.

For almost two weeks, Serena worked sixteen hours a day. At the end of the first day, she took all the papers handed in by the students and did a comprehensive data analysis. She was so attentive that she was immediately able to closely observe the students. Some of them had lost loved ones. Some had been overly stressed. Some were obviously withdrawn. She started to talk to some of them and lent them her sympathetic ear.

On the flight home, I asked her what she had learned.

"Obviously, I gained some knowledge and learned some techniques in psychology, but that is not the most important thing. I learned so much from the people there about perspective. I discovered that I was depressed over things that were of little consequence. These people showed me what is really important in life." Then she smiled widely. "But I think the most important thing I learned is this: I learned about the joy of giving. When I did things to help other people, to make their lives happier and better, I felt an *explosion of joy* inside like I have never experienced before. Giving, helping, and making the world a better place—that must be the meaning of life!"

> *When I did things to help other people, to make their lives happier and* better, I felt an explosion *of joy inside like I have never experienced before.*

Chapter 9

GENTLE FOOTPRINTS

You are not a drop in the ocean.
You are the entire ocean in a drop.
~ Jalaluddin Rumi

Parenting Tours

It felt as if the earth had quaked under me with Kimi's birth. The earth had also quaked under China.

Laying the groundwork for the EAP in China had been a huge step, and I was pleased. Yet I knew China had a long way to go. I was one man, but I also knew that big things could happen as a result of many small footsteps moving in the same direction. I was determined to continue passing on the gift of giving and to try to enact a change in the attitude toward mental health care in China.

More and more calls came in asking specifically for parenting lectures. That didn't come as a surprise. With most Chinese families having just one single child, parents and grandparents were overly-protective on the one hand, and overly zealous on the other, putting enormous pressure on the child to succeed. So many families were hedging their bets that this one child could change the family fortune of the entire clan. While some children did succeed, most came up short. For both, the psychological cost was enormous.

While it seemed that all the family's attention and resources were focused on the one child, there was actually very little attention placed on who the child really was, what he or she liked, and what his or her purpose in life might be. The child's purpose in life was to make the family proud.

> *Today, we have you, a parenting expert, giving a lecture here. No one has ever paid attention to this small town. This has never happened here before. The whole day will be like a festival!*

Word of my parenting lectures went around. Some requests came from the most unexpected places. A few lectures were markedly memorable.

One of the lectures was in a very small town deep in the mountains. The lecture was to take place in the afternoon at the only large venue in town—a movie theater. The organizers took me out to breakfast just across the street from the theater. I saw the square next to the theater filled with people, women in colorful outfits dancing, and a men's percussion ensemble playing.

"This looks like a festival. Is there some other activity going on here this morning?" I asked.

The organizer laughed. "No, not at all. This is a small town where nothing ever happens. Today, we have you, a parenting expert, giving a lecture here. No one has ever paid attention to this small town. No one ever cared about us. But you chose to come here. This has never happened here before. It's the biggest event in town as far back as people can remember. The whole day will be like a festival!"

"But it's only eight in the morning!" I said.

"Yes, but they have nothing else to do anyway. Just wait, there will be more people as the day goes on."

Sure enough, before we finished breakfast, a group of school children showed up and performed dance and martial art exercises. Old men and old ladies performed local opera. Just before noon, dancing lions and local acrobats came. The square was filled with people.

The theater was filled an hour before the start. Everyone inside was given a ticket with a number for prize drawings. Half an hour before the start, it was standing room only. Five minutes before the start, children had to come onto the stage so that they could make room for more people to come inside the theater.

"Mr. Yin, we have planned eight rounds of prize drawings. The grand prize will be at the very end. During the lecture, we need you to plan seven short intermissions for prize drawings," the emcee told me.

"Seven?" I was surprised.

"Yes, seven. We have over two hundred prizes to give away."

"Are they here for the prizes or for the lecture?" I asked.

"For the lecture, of course!" she assured me. "But it's a local tradition that we have prize drawings at events that involve the whole town."

When the lecture started, the adults were mostly silent, but kids were still running around. I needed to get their attention. The best way to do so would be to get the kids involved. As I got on stage, a little boy came running across. I picked him up and held him in my arms.

"How old are you, kiddo?" I asked.

"I'm four." He stuck out four chubby, little fingers.

"Now, let me ask you a question." He looked at me attentively. "I want to ask you which you prefer." I put him down in front of me as I stood over him like a giant. "Would you rather I speak to you like this?" I paused.

He looked up nervously.

Then I squatted down to look at his eyes which were now level with mine. "Or would you rather I talk to you like this?"

"This way!" He smiled and squatted beside me.

I looked at the audience. "Can you imagine standing in front of Yao Ming or Shaq?" The adults laughed. "Well, that's what it's like for kids when you stand in front of them like that. It can be intimidating, and even frightening. They can't relax. As parents, we need to be constantly aware of our children's perspective. Let's start by getting to know what the world is like for them." I went on to describe various parenting strategies which were all foreign concepts to those assembled in this remote area.

The atmosphere inside the theater was vivacious. There was laughter, people shouting their agreement, spontaneous applause, and lots of interaction. The seven rounds of prize drawings were not the unwelcome interruptions that one might expect. At the first interruption, forty modest eighth place prize winners won a plastic cup. That was later followed by pillow cases and umbrellas, with the final grand prize being a mosquito net!

I had the honor of handing the grand prize to our winner. I held the mosquito net and talked to him. "I want to know where will you hang this mosquito net."

"It will be hung over my grandson's bed," he said.

"Now, where is your grandson?" As soon as I asked that, a boy of four or five climbed onto the stage.

I looked at the grandfather. "This prize is actually for him, right?"

> *You have won the grand prize! This is just for you! You will never get bitten by mosquitoes again!*

He nodded.

"I want you to hand this prize to him. But let me warn you. You must do it the right way and demonstrate that you have learned something today. If you do it wrong, I have the power to withdraw the prize."

He started laughing. "Oh, I have learned! I know how to do this!" He squatted down to his grandson's level and spoke softly, "You have won the grand prize! This is just for you! You will never get bitten by mosquitoes again!" The grandson held the mosquito net in his hands and the grandpa hugged him. The crowd exploded into thunderous applause.

The festival at the square in front of the theater continued into the evening. There were even fireworks. I have given lectures in front of nearly ten thousand people in major cities, but nothing beat this small town.

I will never forget the toothless grandmother in the front row, still in heavy opera makeup, who smiled and laughed throughout the four hours. I will never forget the two-year-old twins who hugged my legs like two koala bears hugging a eucalyptus tree, as I was surrounded by audience members after the lecture. But more than anything, I will remember a young teenage girl who picked up a paper heart from the confetti and stopped me as I was walking out of the theater. Accompanied by her parents, she was crying and could hardly speak. She put the paper heart in my hands. "I can't talk. I just want to give you this." Her parents both hugged her tightly. "We are sorry. Now Mom and Dad know better. We love you so much!"

Would You Please be Miserable?

A most memorable exchange came after a morning lecture in the small town outside of Urumqi. I was rushing out to get into the waiting car which was to drive me to my next stop, the oil town of Karamay, about five hours away, for a lecture that same evening. I was stopped by a mother with a young teenage girl. The girl looked to be about fifteen and was crying.

"Mr. Yin, could you give me just a minute? You must help me! I need your help to save my daughter!"

I told my driver, who was worried that we may be late already, to give me a minute. Then I said, "I only have a minute. How may I help you?"

She said, "My daughter thinks she's a lesbian. I cannot accept that! I need you to help me change her back to a normal person! Please! I beg you!"

I looked at her daughter. She was sobbing uncontrollably. I did not have much time. I had to think quickly about what to do.

"Please help change her back into a normal person!" the mother reiterated.

"All right, I will ask you to do something. If you can do it exactly as I ask you, then I will do as you have asked."

"What do you want me to do?" She looked desperate.

"Look at your daughter. She's crying. She looks sad. How does that make you feel?" I asked.

She didn't respond.

Then I said, "Now, I want you to look directly into her eyes and repeat what I say. If you can repeat what I say word for word with no difficulty, I will help you change her," I promised.

> *Your sexual orientation is making me quite uncomfortable. Would you please continue to be sad and miserable for the rest of your life just so that I can be more comfortable?*

The mother nodded.

The daughter continued to sob.

"Don't look away. Look directly into her eyes and say this." I started my sentence. "Dear daughter, I can see that you are crying, and you are sad. But your sexual orientation is making me quite uncomfortable. Would you please continue to be sad and miserable for the rest of your life just so that I can be more comfortable? Please?"

The mother started to repeat after me, but halfway through, she stopped. Tears were streaming down her daughter's face. And now the mother's eyes began to water as well. She suddenly hugged her daughter. Mother and daughter sobbed on each other's shoulders.

"I already know that you love your daughter. I think at this moment, she also loves you more than ever. I wish you both happiness."

At this moment, the anxious driver tapped me on the shoulder and I hopped into the car.

A few years later, I was on a train from Urumqi to Hami. I went to the dining cart for a drink. Walking back I passed a sleeper berth with the door open. Inside were two young women. I immediately recognized one of them as that same young teenager. I stopped and smiled as I looked inside.

She noticed me looking at her. "Sir, do I know you?" she asked.

"Perhaps. I just want to tell you that I am glad to see that you are happy." I smiled and left.

A few seconds later, she came running after me. "Sir, I remember you now!" She caught up with me and held my hands. "I just want you to know that on that day when my mother and I ran into you, I had planned to commit suicide that exact evening. You saved my life." Then she hugged me and began crying.

Tears of happiness sprung to my eyes as well.

The Guqin

One day, a call came in from a complete stranger. I didn't know then, but that call would one day change my life. It was a young government official named Zoe from the small southern city of Quzhou.

Quzhou is a city with a rich history because of its military airport. The airport is famous as the place where Lt. Col. James Doolittle's men were supposed to land their planes after their raid on Tokyo. When Doolittle's men were supposed to land in Quzhou, they discovered that the airport was already under Japanese occupation, forcing the American airmen to crash-land in the rice fields throughout the surrounding areas. This military operation ended up profoundly changing the direction of the U.S.-Japan conflict during WWII.

Those living in Quzhou proudly tell how local Chinese farmers protected and hid the American airmen despite the massive sweeps conducted by the Japanese Army with intentions to dole out retribution to any Chinese who aided the airmen.

"Mr. Yin," Zoe said, "I have worked for a couple of years to organize Quzhou Volunteers Alliance to serve our community. The program is finally ready to be launched tomorrow. We were just discussing how wonderful it would be if we could have a dynamic speaker to speak on volunteerism. A woman there said she had attended one of your lectures before and that you'd be perfect. But we have no budget, and you would have to go to the airport right away if you were to come. I know it's unlikely that this could happen. I just thought I would ask anyway."

"What a wonderful program! I'd love to support it! Do you also need someone to train your volunteers?" I asked.

"Of course! But since we aren't paying you, I don't want to ask too much," she said.

"If it were just a speech, I'd come, but I wouldn't be that excited. Training volunteers is something I'd really love to do. That is something that will make a real difference. Let me book a flight first."

In addition to the speech at the launching ceremony, I would train the volunteers, train the local youth services staff, train the elderly services staff, mentor the local counselors, and train the nursing staff at the local hospital.

"You'd better hurry. There's only one flight that departs from Beijing and it leaves in about three hours!"

Over dinner, we arranged the schedule for the three days. In addition to delivering the speech at the launching ceremony, I would train the volunteers, local youth services staff, elderly services staff, nursing staff, and I would mentor the local counselors.

It was a full schedule, but all the effort was worth it because the project was extremely successful. Over the next three years, I returned to Quzhou each year to follow up on the work we had done.

Quzhou is also famous as the place that produces the best Guqin, which is an ancient zither instrument with thousands of years of history.

Before my departure on the third trip, Zoe wanted to show the gratitude of the town. "Mr. Yin, we don't have money to pay you, but we want to give you something to show our appreciation." I was presented with a beautiful, exquisite, 7-stringed Guqin. "This instrument was made especially for you by the best instrument-maker in the area. It has your name carved on the back."

It was the most beautiful instrument I had ever seen. Music is my special love, and I continue to treasure it.

I developed a special bond to this city of Quzhou. Little did I know then, this bond was planned by the higher intelligence because my footprints would circle back through this city to conduct some truly important work there later.

Sherry: A Crisis Comes Home

For several years, it had been difficult to say what my main area of interest was. My work had included lectures and workshops on a wide range of topics, counseling, community work, TV, radio, magazine columns, and even training for the Beijing Olympics volunteers. But now a new path, a new focus, was about to emerge. It would develop into a new mission: crisis intervention. In this case, the start of the path was intensely personal.

Not everyone is comfortable with crisis intervention. But as a counselor, one knows it comes with the territory. Counselors do not go out of their way to look for crisis. Most times, the crisis comes to the counselor.

Such was the case with my sister, Sherry, who was five years younger than I. Our relationship had been quite different from most brother/sister relationships. She was born in 1968, which was during the Cultural Revolution. I remember one day, during one of those month-long stretches when our parents were forced to leave us alone, I saw her sitting on the bed with her eyes closed and her face leaning against the wall.

"Why are you leaning your face against the wall?" I asked.

"Because it's cool and feels good," she replied.

I put my hand on her forehead. It was hot. She had a fever.

"I need to take you to the hospital. Come on, get ready," I said to her as I went over to the drawer to check how much money I had left. There were just a couple of bills and mostly coins.

"I don't want to move. I don't want to walk," she said.

"I'll carry you on my back. Come on!" I put her on my back and started walking.

I was just a seven-year-old boy. Carrying Sherry and walking a couple of miles was too much for me. I had to stop every twenty yards or so to rest. She was half asleep most of the time. Somehow, I managed to get her there.

Once at the hospital, I went up to one of the staff and said, "I need to speak to the head of the hospital." After being ignored by several people, one of them did get me to the person in charge.

"Please! My sister is sick. My parents aren't home. They won't be back until next month. My mom works at the Beijing #22 Middle School right across the street. If you don't believe me, you can go and check. I don't have much money right now. But I need you to take care of my sister right away. When my mom is back, we will pay you in full for the medicine and treatment. Please help us," I pleaded.

The head of the hospital looked at me. He looked at my sister and felt her forehead. Then he picked her up and held her.

"You are such a sweet angel. You're so lucky to have a big brother who loves you so much." He turned to me and said, "Of course, we will take care of her now. Don't worry."

He called to one of the nurses. "Make sure these two kids are given the best care. Calculate the cost and put it on my desk."

With that, Sherry was seen by a doctor. They gave her a shot to bring her temperature under control. There was a blood test. Half an hour later, the doctor gave us some medication.

"Medication can help cure her, but it can also be dangerous. Make sure you follow the instructions. I wish you had an adult with you." The doctor looked at me, a short and skinny seven-year-old.

Sherry's eyes suddenly popped open. "My big brother *is* an adult."

"Oh really?" The doctor smiled. "I have never met an adult who was so small. Why do you say he's an adult?"

"Because he can do anything. He can always take care of any problems. He takes care of me," Sherry said.

I took Sherry's hand. "Well, we take care of each other," I said.

I have always felt responsible and somewhat guilty about Sherry. When I left for the U.S. at age sixteen, I effectively left all family duties to my eleven-year-old sister. Not only that, but my family could only afford to have one child overseas. Since I was away, it also took away her dreams of studying overseas. By the time I came back, she was already a successful career woman, a wife, and a super mom. And now with me back in China, the family was finally together again.

Everything changed later in 2008. Sherry started having headaches, vision problems, and a variety of other symptoms. At first, she thought she just needed a rest from her hectic schedule. But when I heard about it, I suspected that it might be something more serious, so I convinced her to schedule a consultation with a neurologist. To our dismay, they found a large tumor wrapped around her brain stem. The only treatment was a dangerous and difficult surgery.

> *To our dismay, they found a large tumor wrapped around her brain stem.*

The surgery lasted eleven hours. Several surgeons took turns working on her. "We literally had to peel the tumor off one cell at a time. It was wrapped that tightly around the brain stem. There may be complications, but we won't know for a few days," the head surgeon told us.

A few days later, when the effects of anesthesia and medication wore off, the pain started. It was the most excruciating pain, and it was incessant. We went to several hospitals and clinics and tried every possible procedure. Nothing worked.

The doctors described it as a pain that is a hundred times worse than that of childbirth. With incredible will and determination and the support of family and friends, Sherry persevered. Occasionally she even played the piano. But the pain would not stop. In the backs of our minds, we all wondered how much longer she could hang on.

About six months later, Sherry asked me to come over. We talked for a short while. Then she said, "I know this has been the most unimaginable experience I have ever had. I know it is for you as well. I only have one wish." She paused.

"What is it?" I asked.

"I know you are in the most noble of professions. You may speak modestly about it, but to me, you are in the profession of saving lives."

Then she looked me right in the eye. "Make what I went through, and what you are going through along with me, into something that can help you reach an even deeper understanding about humanity. And if you can use that understanding to save one life, then all that I suffered would not be in vain. My life and death would be given meaning. Then it would be all worth it." She smiled. "I know you can make it worth it. I know it. After all, you are that incredible big brother who can do everything, and since childhood, we have been a team."

We hugged.

"I'm counting on you to make it all worth it," she said.

I didn't completely understand why she said it. In hindsight, I probably did, but I was not ready to recognize it. A few days later, as

I was in another city, I got the call. Sherry's life had ended at the still tender age of forty.

Losing a loved one is something that we all must go through. But witnessing and experiencing Sherry's long, painful suffering process, and then losing her in such a devastating way, was different.

Having done grief counseling for so many years, I was aware of everything that is involved in the trauma and grieving process. But this was personal; this was my first time experiencing the whole mother lode directly and needing to deal with every conceivable aspect myself.

As a counselor, words like "I understand" and "I feel your pain" always sounded trite. But now, as I was on the receiving end, they almost sounded completely insincere. As much as I know people tried, they didn't truly understand, and they didn't truly feel my pain. There was a strange sense of loneliness that descended over me. I wanted to stay away from all those people who wanted to help, even those with the best intensions. Their help seemed counter-productive.

> *There was a strange sense of loneliness that descended over me. I wanted to stay away from all those people who wanted to help.*

Why did this happen to Sherry, to my parents, to Sherry's husband and son, and to me? Why did we have to go through this pain? I had flashbacks of our childhood together. Memories of the past kept playing in my head like an old documentary film. Every time the film was played, different episodes and different stories were recalled and inserted. But every time, the film ended the same way. It ended with Sherry's last words to me:

"If you can use that understanding to save one life, . . . then all that I suffered would not be in vain. My life and death would be given meaning."

In life, we often experience things that are difficult for us to accept, tolerate, or make sense of. This is when we try to search for meaning and make sense of things we that we can't understand. Sherry looked for me to help her make her misfortune meaningful. I felt an obligation to do so. Instead of dwelling on her death, I sought ways to honor her life.

Chapter 10

DESCENT BELOW VISUAL GLIDEPATH

Then the child opened its eyes, and looked up into the angel's beautiful face, which beamed with happiness, and at the same moment they were in heaven, where joy and bliss reigned. The child received wings like the other angel, and they flew about together, hand in hand.
~ Hans Christian Andersen, "The Angel"

Asiana Airlines

On July 6, 2013, I was to give a parenting lecture in the southern city of Shenzhen. I was staying at a nice hotel with access to CNN. In the middle of the night, I woke up and clicked on the television. Immediately, I saw live footage rolling of a damaged airplane with smoke billowing out of the fuselage. I heard the reporter say, "There were at least fifty Chinese high school students led by a handful of teachers on Asiana Airlines Flight 214. They were heading to a summer camp in North America. Unfortunately, the plane crashed on landing. We understand there are casualties."

For the first few seconds, that was all I got. I didn't know where it took place. A chill went down my spine. Around ten hours earlier, my wife, Vanessa, had left to lead a group of students on a summer camp trip to Canada. They should have just landed in Vancouver. There were also around fifty students in her group. Vanessa was one of the handful of teachers who led the group. Could it be? My heart stopped beating. I grabbed my phone and called Vanessa. There was no answer on her cell phone.

I began to pray.

"We understand that the largest group, a group of more than thirty students, were from the southern Chinese city of Quzhou," I heard one of the reporters say.

Quzhou? Did she say Quzhou? I wasn't sure. Quzhou isn't exactly the easiest word for an American reporter to pronounce. I grabbed my phone again and called Zoe, the young government official in Quzhou. My heart started to break for that small city with which I had fallen in love just a few years prior.

The students on board are mostly from the same school in the Jiangshan, a city about an hour from the center of Quzhou.

"Hi Zoe, it's Paul Yin. I just saw on CNN that there was a plane crash with students from Quzhou on board. Is it really from our Quzhou?" I asked.

"Yes, it is! The students on board are mostly from the same school in Jiangshan, a city about an hour from the center of Quzhou. What a tragedy!" She explained that they were headed to West Valley Christian School in California for a summer camp to improve their English. She went on to say, "We know of at least two students who died, but we haven't confirmed their identities yet. At least two more are in critical condition. The mayor is holding an emergency meeting right now. I need to get back in there right away!" She said.

140

My heart had begun to beat again. It was not Vanessa. But it was kids. And I knew everyone involved would need help.

"Wait!" I shouted into the phone, trying to keep her from hanging up. "I know you are concerned about the kids who have died or are in critical condition. But every kid on board that plane will have gone through a traumatic experience. Having a friend die in this crash will only add to the trauma. The parents will be affected. There is the danger of PTSD which could affect them for the rest of their lives. I can help. Even before the kids come back, I need to talk to the parents to help them calm down and handle their stress. I need to train them on how to help their kids.

"They need to understand what PTSD is, what to say and do, and what not to say or do. I need to help train all government and school staff who will be working on this issue. Please go in there and tell them I'm coming. I can get to Quzhou today to connect with the families while they await the arrival of their loved ones! I'm so sorry to keep you on the line, but it's really important—"

"You're just the person we need. In fact, I was already thinking about calling you," Zoe said.

I knew I would need additional help. I had knowledge and experience in crisis intervention, but air disaster is a specialized area. I might encounter issues that were beyond my ability to handle.

I started to reach out to people I knew. Within the hour, I got in touch with Bob Boschert who had counseled those connected to the 1996 TWA Flight 800 air disaster. A fuel tank exploded bringing the plane down shortly after takeoff from JFK in New York City. All two hundred and thirty people onboard perished.

Bob and I talked for a long time. At the end of the conversation, he said, "Paul, you already know all there is to know to do your job. You know psychology. You know crisis intervention. You know the Chinese culture. But most importantly, you have a heart of gold and love for these families. That is more important than anything else. Just tell yourself that you are the most qualified person on the planet to help these families. Call me anytime you need me, and I will be available to you twenty-four hours a day."

I immediately flew to Quzhou and arranged a counseling session with the families who had gathered together. The families of the two girls who suffered fatal injuries, and the families of the two girls hospitalized in critical conditions did not come to the sessions. I was most worried about them, but I had to continue working where I could until they were ready.

I taught a long training session for local volunteers which continued the next day. Training local people was necessary because I knew I couldn't live there continuously for several months. Also, I was a stranger. These local people knew the families, already had their trust, and would be in better position to help.

I was so happy to see many of the counselors I had trained in the past in Quzhou come to the training. Several of them were assigned specific duties to look after those four families who were a high priority. I stressed that they needed to be tactful and respectful of their need for privacy and solitude. I also asked them to bring some neighbors to the next training.

On the following day, I trained the teaching staff at Jiangshan High School. They were the ones who would be with the kids daily once school started up again in a few short weeks. They needed to know how to handle things properly. I taught them about the effects of trauma on things like concentration, memory, and the ability to handle stress. They also needed to be able to tell other kids in their classes about how to help rather than hinder the recovery process.

Overall, my plan was to create a large supportive network to help the families and to help the kids. After three days, something resembling a large supportive network was indeed in place.

A Father's Regret

Within those first three days I was informed that there was a lot of concern about a father of one of the students. The father's friends and family were worried that he might be suicidal. This father was in a unique position since something additional had happened to him which severely complicated an already complicated situation.

I met him in a private room in a local restaurant. He walked in leaning heavily on his brother's arm for support. He was so overcome that he could hardly stand up. A few days before, this man and his wife had dropped their son at the airport to catch the flight for the summer camp in California. On the way home, the father had been driving the car when they were involved in a car accident where the mother had suffered fatal injuries. The father, having just lost his wife, was now hearing about the Asiana Airlines crash.

His son called from California to say that he wasn't badly injured. He described himself as one of the "lucky ones" who suffered only "minor injuries." This boy's sunny disposition and optimism were well-known to the other students and to his local community. He had already begun to interpret this bad experience as something positive. He said to his dad, "Remember how the Chinese saying goes: 'If you escape death unscathed, it's because of great fortune ahead.' I wonder what the great fortune will be. I'll see you soon, and I can't wait to see mom when I get back!"

The boy was close to his mom, but not close to his dad. Already crushed by the loss of his wife, the father couldn't imagine how he could tell his son that his mom was dead. He had lost the courage to live and face what was ahead.

> *People will say that they understand, but you know that they can't possibly.*

He sagged heavily into the chair. I held his hands while he cried. The only thing he could say was "I . . . I can't . . ."

I said nothing. I just kept my hand on his arm. His breath was shallow. He was hardly breathing. Occasionally he'd take a deep breath. I waited until his breathing slightly resembled normal. Then I said: "When someone goes through what you are going through, it hurts. It hurts deeply, in a way that words can't describe. People will say that they understand, but you know that they can't possibly. You feel like the loneliest person on earth. But I do understand.

143

"Not too long ago, I lost my younger sister in extremely painful circumstances. She was still very young, with a long life ahead of her. I lost a sister. My parents lost a daughter. Her husband lost a wife, and her son lost his mother. He was only eight at the time. We did not know how to tell him." As I said this, tears began to fill my eyes. He seemed to realize that here was indeed someone who might truly understood him.

He put his head on my shoulder and started to cry out loud. He squeezed my hands so hard that he was cutting off circulation. There was so much pain and sorrow in his crying. I started to cry, in a way that I hadn't even been able to do when I lost my sister. Seeing that I was crying, he put a hand on my shoulders to comfort me. That's when we both suddenly put our arms around each other. Two grown men experiencing the same pain that only the two of us could truly understand.

I held his hands again. I told him my sister's last words that implored me to use her death as a tool to help others in pain. I told him that I had vowed that her life and death would not be in vain. "Your son needs you. You are all that he has now. We need to get you ready to be the only support that he can count on." I gave him a reassuring pat on his arm.

"But I wasn't much of a father," he said. "I worked in another city. I was an absent father. I don't have much of a relationship with my son." He started crying again.

"I know you feel so much pain from the loss of your wife."

"I feel so much *guilt*. I know my son will blame me," he said.

"Do you know what your wife would want you to do right now?" I asked.

He paused.

"She would want me to do everything I can to make sure that our son develops and grows up to be a healthy young man," he said. "But it will be too hard. I can't do it."

I looked him in the eye, "Yes, it will be hard, but I will be with you throughout this process. We will take one small step at a time.

Right now, you need to feel and experience the pain of your loss. Allow yourself to feel it. Let it all out.

"This is not a sign of weakness. It's a sign that you loved your wife very much. Let's not think about the distant future just yet. Let's just get through the next few days, one day at a time, one hour at a time, one moment at a time. Whatever you can do to help yourself through the next few days, whether it's crying, locking yourself up in a room alone, smashing a few things, whatever, you'll need to do it. Promise me that we will get through the next few days one way or another. I will be here whenever I can be helpful. Let's do this first."

He nodded.

"I'll see you again in a day or two."

He nodded.

"You will be here?"

He nodded.

"But, but I don't see how I can face . . ."

"Let's not even think about that right now. Right now, let's just get through the next few days, one moment at a time, until I see you next time. I know you can do that," I said.

"One moment . . . at a time," he muttered.

I had a few follow-up sessions with this father. In the end, he could walk under his own power, and we were able to talk about specifics of what he needed to do.

"You are a great father," I praised him.

"I don't know about great, but I will be the father that's needed. It's my only reason to live. I can't make my wife's death worthwhile, but I can do the only thing that will allow her to rest in peace and for my son and I to live in peace." Then he held my hands. "And you *will* be there, right?"

"Yes, I will be there."

That night, after the tear-choked meeting with this father, I couldn't get to sleep. Bringing up Sherry was instrumental in getting this man to connect with me, but it forced me to relive the pain of my loss. I started to cry alone in my hotel room.

I needed someone to support me. I wrote an email to Bob Boshert, my friend who had worked on the TWA Flight 800 crash and who had promised me that he would always be there if I needed him.

Moments later, Bob wrote me back.

Paul . . .

We have a saying, "Take care of yourself so that you can take care of others." At this early part of the mission, it is hard to do. I understand, but it is a must!

Get your rest so that you can be of better assistance to the families and for a longer duration. You will be more effective. You cannot erase the tragedy or take away the journey that lies ahead for these people no matter how much you give of yourself . . . rest my friend!

~Bob

At midnight, I also called Gem Yan, the counselor from the "Golden Team" with whom I had done many of the Mental Health China lectures. I needed her to be *my* counselor—to help me heal so that I could face what was ahead. The kids were not back yet. The hardest work was still ahead.

A Time to Grieve

Zoe phoned me to inform me that the city of Jiangshan was planning a welcoming ceremony at the airport followed by a huge banquet to welcome the kids home who were on the plane that crashed. "What?" I shouted into the phone. I was not pleased. "Can I talk to the mayor? They need to change their plans. The only thing the kids and their families want is to go directly home after their ordeal. They shouldn't have to be put through a ceremony and a banquet. This may be what the officials and what the media need, but it is *not* what the families need! We need to put the families first!"

"I disagreed with the ceremony as well," said Zoe, "but the decision has been made. They're already setting up the affair."

"No, don't let them do this!" I shouted into the phone. "Let me make a few calls. I will do everything I can to put a stop to this!" I quickly called the mayor.

"No!" I told the mayor. "You *must* put a stop to this! These kids have been through so much. People have died! You say you want to welcome them home safely. How does that make the families who have lost their daughters feel? These teenagers just want to go home. Their families just want to take them home. You want them to put on a smile and behave appropriately for several hours to accommodate *your* plan? That is selfish! We should be accommodating them, not the other way around!"

> *You want them to put on a smile and behave appropriately for several hours to accommodate your plan? That is selfish.*

The mayor's office should be commended for reconsidering and deciding to cancel the plan for the ceremony and banquet. Not only that, they changed the second part of the students' trip home to train tickets so the kids would not have to get on another plane. The media was not notified of the change and, therefore, did not create a problem for the children or their families. When I met the mayor upon returning to the city, I apologized for shouting at her over the phone. My emotions aside, I had to say that this small-town mayor had been exemplary with her leadership in extremely difficult circumstances. Even though I felt that I had little other choice, I felt bad about my outburst.

The memorial services for the girls who had fatal injuries were to be held on the third day after the remaining students and teachers returned from California. I decided I wanted to talk to every kid and teacher from the group before the memorial services. That was almost forty people. I had hopes that everyone would feel mentally prepared to attend the services. In my opinion, the services were extremely important. For many, going to the services might be the first step toward healing.

I started the "pre-memorial sessions" in the afternoon in a large banquet hall at a local western restaurant. The passengers arrived one after another along with some of their close family members. I told them I could see them individually or in small groups. Most of them were still visibly shaken.

As they saw each other, many of them hugged and cried. A few kids had obvious physical injuries, especially to the neck and back. When they started talking, their voices trembled. Many of them stated that they had trouble sleeping, had frequent flashbacks, and found themselves to be sensitive to sudden movements. Several reported that certain sounds, and certain smells (which was a result of the fire on board) triggered feelings of anxiety and fear.

Overall, they were extremely sad to have lost their friends. I took careful notes after each session. I didn't want to take the notes as they were talking, because I wanted them to see my attention entirely on them, and I wanted to be able to make eye contact at all times. I knew this was only a first meeting. There was still a lot underneath the surface. I gave them all my phone number and room number, and I told them that I would be available twenty-four hours a day.

I wasn't able to see all of the almost forty individuals and their families that day. Seeing over two dozen in one day was overwhelming. I finally finished around midnight. I was totally exhausted.

Alice

One case that was referred to me was that of Alice. Her best friend, Becky, had died in the crash. Alice was injured from the crash. She had trouble sleeping and was heard screaming "Why you? Why not me?" in her sleep. Her father called me and told me that she had been crying all the time and refused to talk to anyone. He said he doubted that she would come see me.

"If she ever changes her mind, I am available any time," I said.

I was at breakfast in the hotel restaurant when I got a call from Alice's father.

"We're at the door of your hotel room. Are you at breakfast?" he asked.

"I'll be right there!" I said.

148

"No rush, please finish your breakfast first. We can wait."

But I knew better. I knew that she was reluctant to come. If there was a chance for her to back out, she'd do so. I ran out of the restaurant and toward the elevator.

I was right. When I went to get out of the elevator on the 5th floor, the family was right there, ready to leave. Alice had insisted on leaving.

"Hi, I'm glad you're here," I calmly reassured her.

When we got to my hotel room, she just sat down and started crying.

"Tomorrow is the memorial service. I can't go. She's my best friend and the only person who truly understood me. We were like each other's shadows—inseparable. Things will never be the same," she said.

I listened to her. Her father said she hadn't spoken to anyone since returning home. But she was talking nonstop now. When she was finished, she collapsed on the table.

I used this quiet space to address her, "Alice, I can see how important Becky is to you. I am sure that Becky appreciated having a true friend like you."

"I loved her like a twin sister," she said.

"Do you think Becky would like for you to be there tomorrow?" I asked.

Alice paused. "I guess. But I'm afraid I will lose control."

"So, deep inside you actually want to go?" I asked.

Alice paused again then said, "That is no way to say goodbye to part of yourself."

"What would be a good way for you?" I asked.

"Her life ended so suddenly. I have so much I want to say to her, and so much I want to... It's between her and me. It's just not right with hundreds of people around and all those speeches. It needs to be special, you know, like Becky was. Like our relationship was."

"Alice, tomorrow morning there will be a large public ceremony. I think Becky would like her best friend to be there. Later, let's also have a small private ceremony, just between you and Becky."

"What do you mean a private ceremony just between Becky and me?" Alice looked puzzled.

"I know you have so much to say to her. I want you to write everything down on paper. Write about how much you miss her, reminisce about the good times you had together, the fun, and any regrets."

"And I might need to apologize for certain things as well . . .," Alice mused.

"Yes, anything and everything. You also want her to rest in peace. You don't want her to worry that her death is ruining her best friend's life. The best way to honor Becky is to treasure her memory and then go on living a good life."

I had her attention now, and she was able to look me in the eye, nodding her head.

> *The best way to honor Becky is to treasure her memory and then go on living a good life.*

"Then, make a most beautiful card, decorate it the way Becky would have liked, with her favorite colors, images, words, designs, and messages. Put the letter inside and seal it all in a special way. Bring it to the ceremony tomorrow. Before the public ceremony, you can have a private ceremony just for the two of you. You can talk to her and, in the end, burn this letter and deliver it to her in the form of the ashes."

Alice suddenly was calm.

"Do you want to read the letter?" she asked.

"No, Alice. The letter will be just between you and Becky. Let's keep it that way."

Alice wiped away her tears, "I want to go home and start writing now." She got up and hugged me. "Thank you, sir."

On the next day, hundreds of people came to the ceremony. Rituals can be a very good way to start the healing process. It allows suppressed emotions to come out.

Alice showed me her letter. We went to a secluded corner near where the memorial would take place and put Becky's framed photo on the dirt.

"Becky, you are my best friend, and I will never forget you. I have so much to say to you; I have written it all in here." Alice placed the beautifully decorated envelope next to the picture frame. "This is between you and me." She kneeled down and lit the envelope.

Alice looked up at me with tears threatening to spill down her cheeks. Then she looked back at the small flame dancing on her envelope and added, "I will do my best to live a long, fulfilling life. It would be the best way to honor you. I love you always!"

Counsel for the Counselor

Exhausted and overwhelmed, I recognized that yet again I needed help. I did have Bob from the U.S. who was available electronically any time day or night. Several other American professionals had held online meetings with me to discuss cases. But I needed real people here with me, on the ground, to help with the caseload. My partner from the "Golden Team" of fifty-two lectures, Gem Yan, had just had a baby and was nursing. She wasn't available. Caesar sent me a message: "Paul, if you tell me to come, I will be there without hesitation."

I was just about to get excited when I saw the location where the message came from. He had been working to win the contract for a project at an oil company. The message was sent from the company. I realized that it was likely that he had won the contract and was just starting the project. So, I called him.

"Caesar, are you starting with the project you told me about?" I asked.

"Yes, sir. But if you need me, I'm sure I could find a way out of it and drop this project," he insisted.

"No, no! That wouldn't be right. I know how hard you worked to get this. You should stay there. I'll try someone else," I said. "But you can be my debrief counselor. This will be stressful work. I will need someone like you to talk to and relieve my own stress so I won't be crushed. Can you do that?" I asked.

Caesar assured me that he would be readily available on the other end of the phone if I should need anything.

Jenny

One morning, a distraught father of one of the teens came to my hotel room.

"My daughter has not spoken to us or anyone else about the tragedy since she came back. I know you said they may suddenly go through tantrums of sorts, but she's not just having a bad temper. She's been snapping at her grandma! She never did that before!"

"Tell me a little more about what's been going on," I said.

"Well, she heard that Becky's ashes were brought back here and she just went crazy. She found out that the ashes were buried in the mountains. She insisted on going to see Becky, but when I offered to drive her there, she refused. She's insisting on going alone! But when I said I must go with her, she started smashing things and screaming like crazy!" The father threw his hands up in despair.

"It's clear that going to see Becky is very important to her. We don't know why yet, but it's definitely important. Can you bring Jenny here? Tell her I want to see her because I want to help her see Becky."

Her father brought her to my room. She sat down crying, not saying a word.

"Jenny, I know it is important for you to go and see Becky. It is probably the most important thing for you right now. Is that correct?"

She nodded.

"You need some private time with her, with no one else around, right?"

She nodded again.

"But your father is worried about you. If I create a plan to ensure your privacy and also make sure your father feels comfortable, would you consider it?" I asked.

She nodded.

"This is how we can do it. Let your father drive you to the foothills. Then you can walk up the trail. He will follow but stay at least fifty yards behind you. This way, your father can see you but won't hear you. Do you think this will work?"

She thought about it and nodded.

I looked at her father. He reluctantly nodded.

"Jenny, I know you are going through a hard time. I understand that. I think you need someone who can understand you. I would like to see you each time I'm in town. Would you come?" I asked.

> *I know you are going through a hard time. I understand that. I think you need someone who can understand you.*

She nodded again.

For the next two months, I saw her a few more times. She never spoke. But she came. Even though there was no two-way communication, I could sense that she trusted me. I knew it would really help her if she could talk things out. So, I talked to her mother to find out as much as I could to see if I could find a possible opening. I always believed that the client holds all the keys. I just needed to find the right key.

"Tell me more about her, please. I want to know everything about her."

Her mother talked for about two hours. I carefully listened to every detail. When her mother left, I still didn't feel as though I could formulate a path to be the most effective counselor for Jenny.

I put on some classical music while I replayed the conversation in my head. Suddenly, something Jenny's mother said popped in my head. I said it out loud to myself: *She's been playing the violin since she was six!*

I called her back. "Can you tell me at what level your daughter plays the violin or understands classical music?"

"Oh, I have no idea. Her father and I know nothing about music. I think she's at a quite high level."

"Can you bring her here during the lunch hour?" I asked.

At lunch hour Jenny walked in, sat down, and, yet again, was obviously not going to talk.

"I want you to listen to this." I handed her the headphones.

Jenny gave me a puzzled look. She put on the headphones. I pressed Play. Slowly, tears started streaming down her face.

She listened to the work in its entirety, roughly twenty-five minutes. Then she took off the headphones.

"This is exactly how I feel. Exactly! How is that possible?"

"That's a violin concerto composed by Alban Berg. The work is subtitled *To the Memory of an Angel*. It was written for a thirteen-year-old girl who had just died. Most people wouldn't call this beautiful music. That's because they don't know how it feels to mourn for a teenage girl who just died. But you know. You don't want to talk to people because you don't think there are people who can understand how you feel. But Alban Berg does, and I do. In fact, there are many people who can understand.

"Loss is part of life. When we experience it, we are sad, disillusioned, and often, we lack the words to express it. But we cannot lock ourselves up in our little world of sadness. We still need to connect with the rest of the world and move on. Music can be your therapy." I handed her my CD player, the headphones, and the CD. "You can start with this. I will carefully select a batch of music just for you. Music will bring you out and help you express your feelings of loss."

The Scars of Memory

I still hadn't had successful contact with the families of the three young girls who had died. I received updates from volunteers and friends about their situation and had been mentoring them on how best to help the families. Unfortunately, they were not ready to work directly with me.

The most important contact for me was Ms. Mao, an English teacher at the school. She was the teacher who was sent to the U.S. by the school right after the crash. She dealt with much of the communication between the U.S. and China and was the trusted contact for all the families, especially the families of the three girls who died and the other girl still in the hospital. This latter girl was by now out of danger but had a long road to recovery ahead.

"These three families have now formed a closed circle. They have no contact with anyone else. I'm starting to get worried about them," Ms. Mao said.

"I think it is good that they have each other for support," I said. "They have similar experiences, so they trust and understand each other."

"But I really want to bring you into the circle. You could help them so much!" she insisted.

"We'll try when the opportunity is right, but I don't want you to seem too pushy. You're the only outsider allowed in the circle. It's important that your position doesn't become vulnerable."

The next afternoon, Ms. Mao called to tell me that the families were inviting me to dinner. I was nervous. I had a feeling that they were only willing to meet me to placate Ms. Mao. This was my one and only chance to establish trust, but I was not exactly in good condition for a meeting. After two days of nonstop sessions, I was severely sleep deprived.

I entered the dining room and immediately felt awkward. Here were three families who had lost their children and in two of the cases, their only child. Everyone's face was cold and expressionless. They mostly avoided any eye contact. Ms. Mao did her best to make me comfortable.

After I sat down and everyone was introduced, Becky's father proposed a toast. "This is to welcome Mr. Yin to our very closed circle. I am not much of a talker. Let's drink!" He gulped down the first shot. I immediately gulped down my glass and turned it upside down to show that I had emptied it. Ms. Mao, who knew I never drank liquor before, looked at me with surprise and was about to say something. I signaled her to stop. I had decided to take on all-comers. This was not an evening to say no.

After a couple of rounds, the talking started.

"This closed circle is necessary. Just yesterday, someone tried to comfort me by saying, 'At least you're lucky that you have another child.' What the hell was that? Was that supposed to be comforting? Ugh!" Debbie's father said, exasperated.

"Forget about them! Let's drink, Mr. Yin," Debbie's mom raised her glass to me. I raised my glass and emptied it again.

I don't know how much I drank. But soon I passed out.

When I woke up, I was on a sofa in the lobby, with a garbage can beside me. I had been throwing up. All three families surrounded me. Becky's dad was apologetic. "Mr. Yin, we didn't know you don't drink. I am sorry. Are you all right?"

I was still a little dizzy. "No, please don't apologize. I wanted to drink. I was sent here by my sister Sherry. She told me to do everything I can to help you. I knew this was my only chance to gain your trust. I wasn't going to say no. I really wanted to earn your trust and be a member of your closed circle."

I really wanted to earn your trust and be a member of your closed circle.

"Well, you have been successful! You didn't need to drink to earn that status, but you are a member of the circle now!" they all agreed. "We are happy to have you join us." Debbie's mom looked around the circle and smiled at the heads bobbing up and down.

I threw up into the garbage can.

"Should we send you to the hospital?" Becky's dad asked.

"I just need to sleep and rest. I hope I can have a chance to talk to all of you before I leave town. Ms. Mao can help schedule it. I need to sleep . . ." With that, I closed my eyes and collapsed back down on the sofa.

I woke up at two in the morning thinking about Sherry. I called Gem Yan and started crying over the phone. I needed to talk to someone. My partner from the Golden Team didn't let me down.

"I know you did this because you knew it was your only chance. This is so you! Look, you can be a hero again tomorrow. But right now, Paul, you can just be like a little kid." Gem knew this was exactly what I needed.

I cried and talked and Gem listened and comforted me until eventually she talked me to sleep.

When I rose for the day, I was greeted with a photo of my little Kimi on my phone. Her hair was in two mussed up pigtails and her eyes were squeezed shut tight. Her two soft hands were clasped in front of her, and she was sitting on the edge of her bed, praying.

Vanessa sent this message to accompany the picture:

I asked Kimi if she misses you. She said of course, because she loves Daddy the best. Then I asked her if she knew why Daddy was away so much lately.

"I just know that my daddy is somewhere helping people. That's what he does."

"But you miss Daddy."

"Yes, but I shouldn't take him away from the people who need him."

"What do you do then when you miss your daddy?"

Kimi closed her eyes and started to pray. That's when I took the picture.

When she'd finished praying, she said, "You know what, all I need to do is to do this. I can feel Daddy right next to me! It's like magic!"

With the prayers of my precious five-year-old upholding me, over the next two days I talked to all three families. I had sessions with each family and then with each individual person separately. I had finally made the breakthrough.

Derek

I continued to get calls to help with even more cases. There were dozens of students from the city of Taiyuan who were also on the plane. I flew there to help.

No kids from Taiyuan had died in the crash. While there were broken bones and such, their overall condition seemed better. But they suffered because they didn't receive proper intervention early on. They were also in an environment where people had little understanding and sympathy for PTSD. Here in Taiyuan, these kids, whose academic performances dipped, were told to "toughen up" and "stop continuing to use the air crash which happened a long time ago as an excuse!"

I met with Derek. He sagged into the sofa and sighed, "Why does this always happen to me?"

I listened to him recounting all his misfortunes. He talked on and on. "I like how you listen to me," he said. "Most other adults would have stopped me long ago with their lecture on how I should think."

"Let's think back to the hotel room in San Francisco right after the crash. You said that's where you felt the most helpless. There were no adults there to tell you what to do. Ready or not, you were more or less on your own. What did you try to do to help yourself?" I asked.

He thought for a moment. "I couldn't sleep. I found this Bible in the room, so I started reading."

"Do you remember which part you read?"

"I have no idea. I think there were some poems. Reading the Bible comforted me. I felt better."

"Have you read the Bible now that you are back in China?" I asked.

"No. But you know what?" He looked around even though we were the only two people in the room. "I stole a Bible from the American hotel. I think I committed a crime, no?" he asked mischievously.

"On the contrary, I think they are happy that you took it," I said. "So, you went through all the trouble to take it, why aren't you reading it now?" I asked.

"The English is a little too difficult for me."

"Why not get a Chinese version. You can easily find one here, you know."

"Well, after reading a few really nice poems, I started back at the beginning and tried to read the whole thing. I thought it was really boring. So I lost interest," he said.

"I think you should get a Chinese version. Then I want you to read, not from the beginning, but go straight to the book of Job."

"What is that book about?" He became curious.

> *Job was a man who ...* *began to ask the very* *question that you keep* *asking.* Why me? Why me?

"Job was a man who met one misfortune after another. So he began to ask the very question that you keep asking. Why me? Why me?"

"Are you a Christian, Mr. Yin?" Derek asked.

"What I believe is not important. The important thing is that you have had a good experience with the Bible, so you already have a head start there. This is about you, not me."

Derek thought for a moment, "I know someone who has a Chinese Bible. I will borrow it and read it."

A month later when we met again, Derek told me excitedly that the Book of Job was exactly what he needed. He felt so much better and now had a totally different perspective on his perceived misfortunes.

Tommy

I was at the airport, ready to board a flight to the U.S., when I received a phone call from Tommy's mother. She was frantic. "My son is hitting his head on the concrete wall repeatedly and he is bleeding! Can you help me!"

She explained to me that Tommy had been having problems at school, but his claim was that none of it was his fault. Just a week ago, Tommy told her about a question that was written into his physics exam:

An airplane was flying at 12,000 meters when the engines failed. The plane started free-falling. What would the speed of the plane be when it hits the ground.

Tommy protested about the question to no avail. He was so upset that he was unable to do the rest of the physics exam. Obviously, his grade suffered. The teacher was angry at him for "continuing to use the air crash as an excuse," and he was repeatedly punished for it. Today, the teacher snapped at him by saying, "stop being a sissy!"

"Let me talk to him."

Tommy came to the phone and screamed. "I'm not a sissy! Why can't they understand me! I'm not using excuses!"

"Tommy, can you tell me who *does* understand you?" I asked.

Tommy calmed down a bit and said, "Well, my family, you, my friends . . ."

"Who are the important people in your life?"

"My family, my friends, and you . . ."

"So, you are telling me that all the people who are most important to you understand you, and the only people who don't understand you are people who are not important to you?" I asked.

Tommy thought for a moment and considered my words. "True. I really can't imagine why I'm hurting myself and the people most important to me because of some stupid thing from the mouth of someone not important in my life."

"Tommy, I want you to find something big and soft. Next time you're angry, instead of hitting your head on the wall, I want you to hit the big soft thing with your fist and kick it with your foot. If you can't find one, I will bring one for you."

Tommy managed a laugh. "I wish you lived in Taiyuan. I would like to be able to see you and talk to you every time I begin feeling frustrated."

"Tommy, I am glad I've been able to help you a bit, but I need to step aside to give you some room to develop yourself. You need that space so you can later say proudly *I did it* instead of *Mr. Yin did it.*

How about if I talk to you again in three weeks. I don't want to hear about a bandaged head. I want to hear you tell me *I did it!*"

Tommy laughed. With that, I hung up the phone and boarded the plane— the last passenger down the jetway.

A New Normal

It took more than a year, but eventually all the kids' lives returned to a new normal. Their academic performances improved. Their health improved. They started to socialize normally and connect with people around them. Most of them were able to get back on an airplane and start traveling. After yet another year, most of them started college—many overseas. It is unlikely that I will ever see them again, but they will always remain part of my life.

The work took so much out of me. For the first time in my life, I started feeling "old." I needed a break. I also needed to get back to some "normal work."

Did that mean back to another lecture tour? Maybe. I started planning halfheartedly. Crisis intervention is important work, and it is exhausting work. I had gained valuable experience, but it's the kind of experience that you never wish to have an opportunity to use again. However, crisis is part of reality.

> Crisis intervention is . . . the kind of experience that you never wish to have an opportunity to use again.

I had been given the opportunity to serve and to gain experience. I had been trained by eight months of hard work following the crash of Asiana Airlines that claimed the three young girls' lives and mentally complicated the lives of many others. There must a reason for that training. Indeed, the world was about to be shaken by another airline tragedy. And this time the help was going to be needed in my beautiful hometown of Beijing.

Chapter 11

HEAVEN'S BREATH

To see a World in a Grain of Sand
And a Heaven in a Wild Flower,
Hold Infinity in the palm of your hand
And Eternity in an hour.
~William Blake, from "Auguries of Innocence"

MH370

Close to eight months had passed after the Asiana Airlines 214 disaster. On March 8, 2014, I was ready to put that experience to use for another airline disaster that was unprecedented. On that day, the Lido Hotel housed the bewildered and broken-hearted family members and loved ones of the two hundred and thirty-nine people on board.

The hotel lobby was crammed to capacity with families of MH370 passengers. I slowly walked through the crowd. The heavy weight of their despair settled squarely on my shoulders. I noticed an elderly lady sitting on the floor who was crying. I sat down beside her while tears began rolling in single streams down my cheeks. I held her hands, and I closed my eyes; she put her head on my shoulder and started crying louder. I wrapped my arms around her to comfort her. She cried and cried and her shoulders shook.

I moved to the next person and I held that person's hands. My own tears flowed freely. In a sea of strangers, having someone caring to be with them at their darkest moment was what these people needed. I also knew that I was going to need more help. A lot of it.

This was a moment that would prove that Sherry's life and death were not in vain, and that all my efforts insisting that there *was* a place for psychology in China were necessary. It felt like every single moment I had experienced in my life thus far had prepared me for this exact moment in time. Gwen; Dr. Frank; Paul, the ticket man; Rudy; the visa officer; my professors—every connection with every person I ever met was a connection I needed to make to prepare me for this moment.

I called Caesar immediately. "I'm at the Lido Hotel," I said. "I'm guessing you're here too."

"Yes, sir. I'm in the lobby. I owe you one, so I have to be here since I couldn't help you during Asiana."

"Do you see the Starbucks?" I spied the green and white sign glowing above the crowd that had assembled around the hotel, and I walked briskly toward it. When I noticed Caesar's familiar gait coming toward me, I hit "end" on my cell.

"Caesar! I'm so glad you're here." I hugged him tightly and slapped his back. A rush of emotion came over me. I had been hoping for an opportunity to again work with Caesar. I knew he would be perfect to have by my side.

Behind us, I heard a familiar voice shouting from the curb, "Paul! Caesar! I knew you'd both be here!" We looked in the direction of the voice. It was Gem Yan, just getting out of a taxi. With her was Lily Zhang. What were the chances? The Golden Team of psychologists from my fifty-two lecture series was reunited! And this time we also had Caesar!

There were a few outdoor tables. The four of us sat down for a quick meeting. We needed to keep clear heads amid the deep despair and chaos surrounding us.

No one had an exact count yet, but Gem estimated, "There must be more than a hundred families here. Let's each take a couple of them and stick with them. How about if these Starbucks outdoor tables act as our "headquarters"? We can check in here once in a while, so we can share information, discuss cases and, if needed, mentor each other."

Suddenly it got quiet. Gem just shook her head and tears welled up in her eyes. "Can you imagine if it was your own family?" she whispered.

The rest of us looked down at the table and blinked repeatedly to hold back our own tears. We were imagining the worst along with everyone else. We had no words.

Lost Legacy

The disappearance of Malaysia Airlines flight 370 prompted the most extensive aviation search to date. As one hundred and fifty-three of the two hundred and thirty-nine passengers were Chinese, it also presented China with the sobering truth that psychological intervention was something that was a necessity.

One hundred and fifty-three Chinese families lost a loved one. Some lost more than one loved one.

Suddenly I was struck with the very real fear that there was about to be a staggering number of suicidal grandparents in the Lido Hotel.

Since most Chinese families have only one child, having both the son and grandson perish together is unthinkable. For most Chinese elders, their children and grandchildren are their reason for living. Their entire life revolves around their offspring. Suddenly I was struck with the very real fear that there was about to be a staggering number of suicidal grandparents in the Lido Hotel.

David and Vivian were a couple around the age of sixty. Their only son, his wife, and their grandchild were all on Malaysia Airlines Flight 370. Vivian was devastated and had been hysterical saying she wasn't going to live anymore if her family members were confirmed dead. David felt compelled to be strong to support his wife, but he was also near the breaking point. A host of uncles (Vivian's brothers) had just arrived. I readily agreed to meet with them.

An uncle came to the door, visibly upset. David and Vivian had locked themselves in one of the rooms. I gathered the uncles together, and I tried to offer them some strategies to keep David and Vivian from experiencing a severe breakdown. I told the uncles, "Officially, the plane is only missing. It may be a long time before we have an official confirmation one way or the other.

"We must prepare for the worst. It may be tempting to try to comfort them with hope. But telling them to hold on to a thin ray of hope is a dangerous thing to do. It may be setting them up for a fall that they can't handle. We need to build a support system around them made up of people they trust. That means you. I will need to train you to be that support system for them during this incredibly difficult time. I'll be here whenever you need me."

The oldest uncle grasped both of my hands in his. "We don't know how to do this. We need you." His own grief was showing in the lines on his face and the tears in his eyes. I ignored the pain of empathy that was beginning to pull at my own heart making its way down through my joints. I needed to be efficient. There was work to accomplish.

I gave the uncles a half hour training session. They listened attentively and took notes. I told them, "Vivian is the one we are mostly worried about right now. But in time, David will likely become the one who becomes more vulnerable. Don't let his apparent strength right now fool you. He's doing what he needs to do as a husband. He's forcing himself to be strong right now, but it may soon become too overwhelming. Please observe him closely. If you notice anything of concern, call me."

Just then, David came out. He took my hands and I hugged him tightly. I could feel his body start to shake as he began to cry like a baby on my shoulder. I squeezed my eyes shut as my own tears threatened to spill over.

"That's okay. It's okay to cry," I comforted him. "I know you feel like you need to be strong for your wife. You may not want to cry when she's around, but you need to let it out. We're all men in this room. We don't need to put on a mask and act." The uncles also came over and we cried together.

"I understand that I need to be strong for my wife, but who will take care of me?" His question came out in a whisper. His eyes could not meet mine; he was so broken. I assured him that I would be there.

Jason

I returned to the hotel lobby, making myself available to people who needed help. As I turned around, Jason was standing right in front of me. This young man had actually been a client of mine in the past. He looked stunned to see me.

"What brought you here?" I asked him.

"My childhood buddy, Luke, and his wife were on that plane. I'm here with several buddies to be with Luke's parents. I was just telling my friends that we need to get in touch with you. And here you are!"

I already knew that Jason thrived on contact with his close circle of friends. These buddies of his were considered family to him.

I asked him about Luke's parents, and he informed me that Luke's mother was on the verge of a mental breakdown.

"Does Luke have kids?" I asked.

"Yes, they have two kids. One is staying with his parents, and one is with the in-laws."

I breathed a sigh of relief. "If the grandchildren are all right, the grandparents should be okay. They can provide companionship and comfort to each other. What's most important at this moment is making sure they have someone with them at all times."

"Yes, that's why we're all here." Jason then introduced me to the gang. There was at least a half-dozen of them.

"Later this evening, I will find time to give you some training. Together, you all will form the support system that they will need to go through this crisis." A half-dozen heads nodded sorrowfully.

Psychologist Uniform

My cell phone rang. It was a friend of my family named Steven.

"We have these dear friends, Sam and Cindy, whom we have known since we were toddlers. We're almost like family. Their son, daughter-in-law, and grandchild were all on that flight. We need help!"

I immediately went to find Steven. He was certain that Sam and Cindy were close to committing suicide. I assured Steven that Sam and Cindy should be safe until a verdict would be made clear in regards to the fate of the plane. I emphasized that he needed to call me immediately if the flight was declared to be fatal.

At one point, as I was heading back toward Starbucks, a gentleman stopped me.

"Are you the psychologist?" he asked.

"Yes, how can I help you?" I said.

"My brother and his entire family were on the plane. My mother, Grace, is inconsolable. I was just talking with friends about this and a man told me that you can help us."

"How did you know it is me?" I asked.

"Well, he said you wear a leather jacket, with a red and white Arsenal scarf and use a walking cane." He pointed at my cane.

I had had a recurrence of joint pain that day and had brought my cane with me when I left for the hotel. This cane, scarf, and jacket were to become my "psychologist uniform" for several weeks.

"I'm here for you. Let's go."

I made my way to the Starbucks with Caesar, Gem, and Lily. Our makeshift team of psychologists held a group meeting.

Some information was slowly becoming available, but a lot of it was inaccurate and confusing. This problem opened the door for conspiracy theories, and this was devastating for the grieving process of all involved. The families desperately needed a starting point for recovery.

"Right now, technically, the situation is that we still just have a missing plane," I said. I was trying to make sense of it. "We have no idea when and if the plane will ever be found. That makes it excruciating for the families. They're in limbo. The problem is that there isn't an appropriate emotion for this. They will cry and then, realizing that this is not a confirmed air disaster and their loved ones may not be dead, they will try to grasp onto hope. But a while later, they realize that with every passing minute the hope seems gone, so they fall back into despair. They will continue through this roller coaster until there is some sort of concrete resolution."

"I heard many are trying to use hope to help them," Lily said.

"Or, more accurately, they are clinging to rumors and conspiracy theories," said Gem.

"That's because they don't want to believe their family members are dead," Caesar said. "They are trying to withhold their grief, but that strong emotion must be released in some way. That grief often manifests itself as anger against the airline, against the government, and against those people made into suspects by the conspiracy theories."

"Are we in agreement that we could potentially have many suicidal people here?" Gem asked.

Everyone nodded.

"But they all say that they won't do it unless and until the crash is confirmed," Lily said.

"I have a mother with a baby. She said if the crash is confirmed, she'll kill herself and take the baby with her." Caesar said that last part quietly.

There was silence. How would we handle the possibility of dozens of suicidal people at the same time?

"We need to start setting up contingency plans for that day, or that moment, when many people may become simultaneously suicidal," I said. "We need more people—not to be here the whole time, but people who can be on call when we need them, even if just for a couple of hours."

"Let's all round up some people to help," Caesar said.

"Better yet, find people within the inner circle of close friends to do the job. That would be most effective. The key is to train and establish an effective support system for each family from within their personal trust circle."

"Great idea," Gem said. "This is going to be a lot of work. I'm wondering how your leg is doing, Paul? Are you able to take this on?"

It throbbed a bit. "Not too bad. But I think this jacket, scarf, and cane will be my uniform as long as I'm here in the Lido Hotel. It will make it easier for people who need me to find me from word of mouth. When I'm not working on a case, I'll walk around the area or sit right here outside of Starbucks. I need to be a visible presence."

"I'll try to be here every other day for a couple of hours," Gem said.

"I'll be here every day if I can," Lily added.

"Same here," Caesar said.

"And I will be here every day all day," I said. We were waiting for a virtual volcano to erupt. I took a deep breath.

Training Jason and His Buddies

At dusk I met Jason and his buddies in the park. Jason's father was also there. "I'm about the same age as Luke's parents, and we have known each other for almost thirty years. They still see Jason and his friends as kids, but I'm someone they can talk to," he said.

"I'm so glad you are here." I stepped quickly toward him and embraced him. Jason's father was exactly the person I needed to be in their circle of trust to facilitate healing. I began training Jason, his buddies, and especially Jason's father to be effective grief counselors.

170

After the training was over, I started walking back toward Starbucks. Jason caught up with me and walked beside me. He asked if we could talk alone in the room he had reserved. Once we entered the room, Jason hugged me and cried inconsolably. It was painful for me to see this strong, fit youthful man crumpled so weakly in this moment of anguish.

When he finally calmed down, he said, "I really need to talk with you!"

I sat down, and he made some tea.

"I talked to Luke last night before he boarded the plane. The last words he said to me were *See you at the game!*"

"Game?" I asked.

"Yes. I got tickets to a game and we planned to go together, just like we used to. That scene plays over and over in my mind, and I don't think I'll be able to even watch another game." Jason started to cry again.

I spent some time talking to Jason. I didn't try too hard to help him get over his immediate pain. I knew that would take time. Right now, he just needed a little comfort.

Seeking Counsel

The first day was finally over. I got in my room at midnight and got online to talk to Bob.

"Bob, this MH370 situation is so overwhelming. I am still in the process of finding out what to do. I need your help!"

Bob replied, *"Paul, this case is unprecedented. No one knows what to do. But you are there. Right now, you are the number one expert on this case. You were sent there because you are the one person who can help these people. Trust in yourself. Trust in your ability. But first and foremost, trust in your heart."*

Conspiracy Theories

For the next few days, the suspense of waiting for the other shoe to drop, while holding onto the thin thread of hope that it wouldn't, was almost too much to bear. Rumors and conspiracy theories abounded. There were believable reports of people from the flight being discovered on lifeboats off Vietnam.

There were reports that people had spotted MH370 flying low in areas way off from its intended course. I had to wonder who these people were who would go to so much trouble to write such a piece of fiction? Then there was "news" that the plane was found intact, having landed somewhere in central Asia. What were the motives of these people? America, Russia, China, Malaysia, the CIA, and ISIS all took turns being the antagonist.

Most of the families grasped onto these rumors and theories like lifelines and held lengthy discussions about the possibilities. I went around seeing all the people with whom I had already established contact. I had to be careful. On one hand, I didn't want to be the one to pour cold water on every ray of hope that they saw. On the other hand, I didn't want them to make too much of it or to be drawn in by the gravity of a conspiracy theory group that was in the process of forming. It did seem as though the families were dividing into two groups: those who were beginning to accept that their loved ones were gone, and those who were holding onto rumors and theories.

Malaysia Airlines held a press conference open to the families daily. But the update sessions became a place for people to vent their misguided anger. Too many people began to be convinced that there was a "truth" that was being withheld from them. "Give back our loved ones! We demand the truth!" became their mantra.

There were complaints about how things were handled by all sides, including the governments of China and Malaysia as well as the airline. But what could they do? It was an impossible task. Any attempts at doing something was seen as an attempt at a further cover-up. Malaysia airlines offered to give each family some money, but most families refused because it was seen as an attempt to force them to accept that their loved ones had died. "They're still alive! Stop covering up!" They would shout.

Inside the hotel suites and rooms where the families were staying, the tension was mounting. Some people were glued to the TV, where there was only the same information and analysis being played repeatedly. The news anchors announced eerily that the pilot's last words were: "All right, good night." That turned out to be untrue, adding to the distrust felt by the families. Tension was high.

> *All right, good night.*

At one point, the news stations proclaimed that the plane had been hijacked. It had landed in either Northern Pakistan or some other central Asian country. The room erupted into cheers. It's hard to imagine people so desperate that they'd celebrate a hijacking. "They're alive! There is hope! Yes!" Their cheers rang out.

I had to work hard to restrain myself from immediately dispelling this rumor. I had to allow it to run its course. I waited until they eventually figured out it was a rumor. And when they did, half of the people sank back into despair, and the other half into anger, convinced that it was just another conspiracy to cover up what had really happened.

The most important thing for me was to maintain the trust that I had established with them. I needed that trust to prepare for the inevitable moment of truth.

Back at Headquarters

Yes, the moment. That's what we talked about at our meeting. "This cannot hold on for much longer," Caesar said. "Things will get out of hand. There soon must be an announcement of some significance. We're preparing for and waiting for that moment." He was right on target.

"When the announcement is made," I observed, "it needs to be meticulously designed—every detail. I'm not confident that Malaysia Airlines can do that. But let's just hope they don't mess it up too much." But I had a bad feeling.

"Is there something else we can do now?" Caesar asked.

"Not much. We prepare and wait. Healing starts with the announcement, regardless of the content or how it's delivered," I said.

"What do you mean?" Caesar asked.

"Even the lowest point can be a starting point for recovery and healing. The problem right now is that there *is* no starting point. And I mean, not just to start healing. They don't even have a starting point for grieving, for sadness, for guilt, and for a host of emotions to properly come out and be processed.

"But whatever happens, these people need a starting point, no matter how low, so that we can help them to start the process of getting better and   rebuilding their lives." I paused. "People were cheering for rumors of hijacking, but the news they dread the most may be the very thing that they need to hear. And that will be extremely painful."

This case wasn't like any other I had experienced. I was mentally and physically exhausted. My joints seemed to be absorbing the pain of the people in that hotel.

I recalled an incident that occurred at a moment when I was particularly overwhelmed with the trauma that surrounded the Asiana Airlines crash. I was hastily grabbing breakfast at a hotel buffet when a Buddhist monk walked by and said, "Sir, you are a man of kind heart."

I thanked him, and he responded, "In fact, you are doing work to save people right now. But you are overextending yourself, and you have gone over your limit. You can't help people if you break down."

After that, he gave me a bracelet of Buddhist beads. "This will help protect you for now. But do take better care of yourself. You will be blessed."

As I shook my head back into the present, I looked down at those very beads. I had worn them ever since that day, and I needed protection and blessings right now.

The Media

"Paul, several people from the media have asked for interviews, and I think you'd be the best person for it. I think you have the best English and understanding. Do you want to do it?" Gem asked.

"You know, I've been thinking about this. I've been staying away from the media. They've all been trying to find families to interview or film. It's creating quite an annoyance. Most families hate it, but the more extreme members of the families are actually looking to get interviewed. That doesn't give a balanced view of how things are." I thought for a while.

"The media has a job to do. I think I should start working with the media just to provide some information to them about how the families are doing. That way they wouldn't have to go after the families and bother them. It would also give the viewers a more balanced view."

I started granting interviews, giving the global audience updates on how the families were doing. I did a fair amount of analysis so that audiences would be able to understand and appreciate the families' reactions, rather than seeing them as being unreasonable and extreme.

I tried to help people understand that this was not just an aviation crisis or a political crisis. It was a human crisis. There were actual human beings involved in this unprecedented incident. I explained those people included not just the families and friends, but also the airline, the governments of many nations, the helpers, and the media.

I tried to help people understand that this was not just an aviation crisis or a political crisis. It was a human crisis.

After one interview, where I had explained the very real and personal plight of these family members, I noticed a cameraman who was especially moved. I hugged him as he became overcome with emotion. But, of all these people, it was the families of those on the plane who were going through unimaginable suffering.

Dropping the Other Shoe

That other shoe dropped suddenly and in the most surprising way. I was sitting at our Starbucks headquarters with Caesar when we saw families begin flocking toward the hotel conference hall. Most of them were smiling and chatting.

"What's going on?" I asked one of them.

"They found the plane!" I was told by the first person.

"It's not official yet, but I think they'll announce it! It starts in ten minutes!" a second person added.

"How do you know?" I asked.

"We got a text message!"

Caesar and I were confused.

Another person showed us the text message. It was in English. It simply said that there will be an important information release and all families were asked to come to the conference hall.

I looked at Caesar. "Today is the day. Let's get ready. Call everyone here."

"Why are they all assuming the plane has been found?" Caesar asked.

"I guess there have been a lot of rumors like that over the past two days." I did wonder, though, why this message was in English. Most of the families didn't know English. How sloppy to send a message in English! I commented to Caesar, "I bet that some of the family members know a little English and simply interpreted this as official confirmation of *good* news. The rest simply accepted that interpretation."

Inside, the official announcement was made. They said that they had *not* found the plane, but that the final verdict was that the plane had crashed. That was the news everyone was dreading. The families erupted. I heard crying, shouting, screaming, and frantic members of the media gathering, rushing in, rushing out, and some following families. One elderly mother screamed and collapsed on the ground. "My whole family is gone!" she cried out. The anguish on her face was heart-wrenching. Her heart was broken.

Several TV cameramen gathered around, pointed their cameras at her face, some literally within a foot or so. However, I saw one Chinese media person pulling his cameraman away.

"Don't shoot this!" he yelled.

"But we were told to get this on camera. That's our assignment!" the cameraman protested.

"I would much rather that my boss think of me as an incompetent reporter than to look into the mirror and think of myself as a scum!" he screamed at his cameraman.

Two people were wheeled out on stretchers and had to be taken to the hospital. There also was a man who jumped down an escalator.

Quite a distance away, two German crews waited. One of their journalists came out of the meeting to talk to them, but they kept the camera pointed away from the families. These two TV crews from Germany had decided to send only one journalist inside without the camera, then film a report without pointing the cameras at the families. I was impressed by their humanity.

Our War Saves

Gem arrived later, so the four of us had a brief meeting. It was freezing outdoors. And it was late. My knees were hurting immensely, but we had to maintain this headquarters, especially now.

I got an urgent call from Steven. He frantically told me that Sam and Cindy were insisting on going out for a walk at midnight alone. He feared that they were about to carry out their promise to self-harm if the plane crash was confirmed.

"It's okay. Stall for five minutes and then let them go. I'll have someone follow them from a distance." I hung up the phone and immediately sent two volunteers. "Listen, just follow them from a distance, close enough that you can see them but don't be too conspicuous." The two people took the instruction and left.

Caesar got a message on his phone. "Paul, I have to go and check on the mother who said she'd take her son with her if the crash is confirmed. She just messaged me."

Gem left to check on one of her clients.

Lily left to check on another elderly couple.

I was left at headquarters alone. Because I had trained a support system for all my clients, I was able to do a lot of the work remotely—via text or phone. They'd report to me whenever there was a new development. I would give them some advice and, more often than not, just words of encouragement.

At around two in the morning, a reporter sat down beside me.

"You are the psychologist?" he asked.

"Yes, sir. Tough night," I said.

"Indeed. I've been a war correspondent. I've seen the carnage of war, but the past few hours were some of the most devastating moments I have experienced as a reporter. I need a chat."

We talked. The talk was repeatedly interrupted by phone calls, text messages I needed to reply to, and voice messages which often turned into long discussions.

"You're like a commander in a war," he said.

"Wars kill. Our war saves," I replied.

"Can anyone save them? So many of them?" he asked.

> *Can anyone save them? So many of them?" he asked.*

"We can't save everyone. We can only do one at a time. You've heard the saying that one shouldn't miss the forest for the trees. Now we need to do the opposite—ignore the forest and save as many trees as we can."

A Starting Point

Two hours later, Sam and Cindy returned safely to their hotel room. Everyone breathed a sigh of relief.

But the friends in their support group told me about a new development. Sam and Cindy were contacted by the conspiracy theorists to join them on a "protest march" on the Malaysian Embassy. They had started actively recruiting people to not accept the "lies" and fight to the end for the "truth."

I chose my words carefully. "I would prefer that none of them go to that march or join that group. However, if going or joining is the only thing that would sustain them—if they couldn't continue with life unless they go or join, then who are we to tell them no?"

"So, should we stop them from going?" one of them asked.

"As I said, it would be better to start healing now, but it may be that going to the protest march is the only thing that will give them a reason to live for one more day. If that is the case, then they should definitely attend."

Apart from Sam and Cindy, none of the families that I had worked with went to the protest march. Early minimal intervention plus training and establishing an effective support system truly worked. It seemed most families who went were those who used hope as their only savior and self-delusion as their only refuge.

Back at headquarters, Caesar approached me with another cup of coffee. Caesar had changed a lot from the time I had first met him right when the EAP was getting its footing in China. I could still see the charismatic, bombastic fellow, but now some years were showing on his movie-star face, and his tone had muted a bit. One thing that remained was the haunted look in his eyes. I knew he had a troubled past.

"Caesar," I said, "I know that you've had things in your past that continue to haunt you. I believe that you can and have been using that pain as fuel to help others." I took a sip from my coffee and then made eye contact with him. "The conspiracy theorists are meeting in the conference room shortly and I would like you to join them. I think that you are the best one from our team to go in there."

When Caesar returned from the meeting, he sought me out. I had just returned from CNN and the Anderson Cooper Show. Caesar handed me a fresh cup of coffee and asked if I could sit with him for a minute.

He folded his hands on the table in front of him and took a deep breath. "I know you've probably heard unsavory things about me.

Those descriptions are probably somewhat accurate. The truth is, I'm simply afraid to face real, genuine, human emotion. It scares me. It's so much safer to play a role and map out plans . . . but this time, we're in a situation where no one can escape from genuine emotion. In the process, I feel that I'm beginning to have the courage to see the real me and to see the real me with all my faults. I think I'm ready to embrace all the things from which I have been running away." Caesar nonchalantly wiped the corner of his eye with his fingertip.

"Caesar," I said, "this is the most important training you will ever experience. I'm impressed by your dedication. The families that you've touched here need you and your insight."

For some of the families at least, a "starting point for healing" had been established, and it was time to start healing. The four of us held another meeting at the headquarters.

"I know this is not a firm starting point for healing to begin," I said, "but for many of the families, even though they may not be truly willing to accept it, they can no longer tolerate the suspense anymore. Now we can start doing some real work."

"I think we have all started doing it. But it's still hard." Lily looked up at the rest of us.

"The Chinese concept of closure, of finality, is markedly different from the western one," Gem said. "They need something concrete. In ancient China, when they couldn't have the body, they'd need at least something from the person from the time he perished—a lock of hair, a piece of clothing, a necklace—to hold a proper funeral and symbolic burial. In this case, we have nothing." Gem understood this concept so well. She had such an amazing way of putting herself in the other person's shoes.

"Good point," I said. "We don't have anything. We don't have the solution to this. But I always believe that the solution is within the person we are trying to help. We need to be patient and observant, so that we can find and seize the opportunity when it presents itself."

"I have found that most of these people are tired," Caesar said. "A part of them wants to hold on to hope, or at least they feel that letting go would be a betrayal. But another part of them wants to start healing. However, the reasons so far are not compelling enough." He spoke slowly, from his heart.

"Right! We need to help them find it. We can't create it and give it to them. We need to find it in them!" I said. "For example, Luke's parents still have their grandchildren. The solution for them is their conviction to holding on to the grandchildren. If they don't start planning for a custody battle, they may lose the children forever to the in-laws. This is the solution and it is within them."

I looked around to each member of the new Golden Team. Each head was nodding in agreement.

It's Within You

Finding these opportunities takes great patience and careful observation of details.

I went to see Sam and Cindy. This was the first time that I had sat down with both at the same time. I allowed them to talk without me interrupting or attempting to interject anything. I was listening carefully and observing.

Then I noticed something—a strand of Buddhist prayer beads on Cindy's left wrist. I looked at Sam. He also had his string of prayer beads on his left wrist. The only major difference was that hers were worn, possibly indicating that she was a Buddhist. Her husband's, however, was clearly new, possibly indicating that he had just received it. Most people in China are not religious *per se,* but at time of crisis, people do tend to gravitate toward religion.

I saw my opportunity, and I immediately decided to seize it.

"Where do you think your son is right now?" I asked Cindy.

She didn't answer at first. I assumed she was struggling with whether to accept that he was already dead.

"My son is now on the other side, I think," she said finally as she took her prayer beads off and started to manipulate them in her hand.

"I'm not so sure," I said.

"What do you mean?" she asked in surprise.

"For someone to go to the other side, he needs to let go of everything in this world, but your son can't do that. He sees his parents suffering. He can't go to the other side. Your son needs your help." I looked directly at her and I leaned forward.

Her eyebrows lifted ever so slightly as she began to understand where I was going. "My son needs me. I will do anything for him," she replied softly.

"You need to start healing and promise your son that you will live a good life. By starting the healing process, you will be continuing your role of being a good mother."

I wasn't telling her anything that she, as a Buddhist, did not know. But these were things that had no meaning when she first learned them, so she forgot them when she needed them. Now, suddenly, she was beginning to understand.

"You're right. I need to get back to being a mother."

I realized something about myself, and about humanity, and maybe even about the field of psychology. I didn't have to share the religious beliefs of someone in need. I just had to be open and observant of who this person was in order to help them find their own unique path to healing. I had found that space for Cindy to begin her healing journey.

Wedding Plans

Caesar called. There was a young man who was planning to get married who needed our help. His parents had been on the plane. Now he was refusing to get married.

"Can you talk with him," asked Caesar. The young man was in his mid-twenties. He felt it might be better for me to work with him since I was older.

He came in with his fiancée. He was emotionless, and she was crying. They sat down.

"I only have a few minutes," he started by saying. "I know you're here to try to talk me into going through with the marriage. But I can't have a wedding without my parents. Unless they find them and they can be present, I will never get married."

His fiancée continued to weep and dab at her tears with a tissue.

I dislike so-called "reasoning." It's the most self-righteous but useless tool. I had no solution to this situation. I needed to look for the solution within him. "Tell me about your parents. I want to know them," I said.

"My parents are the most wonderful people. They are well-educated, classy, elegant, intelligent . . . I could go on and on with complimentary descriptions."

"Were they on a business trip together or was it vacation?" I asked.

"My parents have a passion for world travel. They have traveled around most of the world. This was to be their next to last trip," he told me.

"Next to last? What do you mean?" I was puzzled.

"I was going to get married. My parents decided to have two more trips. Then they would stop traveling," he said.

"Why is that?" I asked.

"They wanted to host my wedding and then get ready to raise grandkids," he said.

I immediately sensed an opportunity. "This was to be their next to last trip. Do you know where they planned to go for their last trip?"

"Yeah, I do. Why?" he asked.

"Well, I have an idea." I leaned closer to him. "Travel was your parents' passion. They had this plan to travel the world. Only one stop was missing. Why don't you complete the journey for them?"

His eyes lit up.

"How about the two of you travel that last leg on their behalf. Take your parents' framed photo with you. Go to all the places and scenic spots where they would have gone. Make their journey around the world complete."

He bit his lip and shook his head. "But . . . I still don't want a wedding without my parents. I don't want to have to smile and laugh and act jovial for hundreds of guests. You know how Chinese weddings are. It's like a carnival circus show. I can't possibly be part of that right now!" he insisted.

"You don't have to do it that way. You can design a wedding the way you and your parents would have liked."

"What do you mean?" he asked.

"Now, imagine this. After you've completed your parents' wishes for a complete journey around the world, how about if you pick a special place that would be meaningful for just the two of you. Maybe it would be at the last stop, maybe at one of your parents' favorite places, or one that is special for you—a spiritual place like a mountaintop, or a secluded valley, or in a canoe—whatever.

"The two of you, and possibly a small handful of people special to you, hold a special spiritual wedding ritual designed by you. There will be no one invited out of courtesy or cultural protocol. In this very private and personal ceremony, you can tell your parents that you have completed their wish by finishing the last leg of their travel. Then, with their blessings, you would be completing their other wish, which is for you to start your own family. These are the only two things left that were of real importance to your parents. Make their wishes come true!"

"They'd certainly be there." He looked like he was already imagining the special wedding in his head.

"Yes, they will be. And they will be pleased and proud," I said.

"Okay. Wow! This just might work," he said.

"You can complete the details later, but I think we are onto something."

Anastasis

Before I left the Lido Hotel, an elderly lady saw me and walked straight up to me, smiling. She hugged me. "I guess you don't recognize me?" she said. I shook my head. "On the first day, I was sitting on the floor crying and you sat down beside me." I looked at her and vaguely remembered the face.

"How are you now?" I asked.

"I am a bit better now. This has been a heart-wrenching roller-coaster, but the most difficult time was that first day. I couldn't see living beyond that day. I could only see darkness ahead. Even though you didn't say a single word to me, your sitting next to me, crying with me, and letting me cry on your shoulder meant so much. I saw you many times later, but you were busy, so I decided not to bother you." She paused and breathed deeply. "I will be leaving soon to go home and take care of my other grandson." She was still smiling, but tears filled her eyes. "Life must go on."

> *She was still smiling, but tears filled her eyes. "Life must go on."*

We hugged again.

As I walked away, I had a spring in my step. My joint pain was gone, and within my heart was a tiny explosion of joy. I knew we didn't do much in the first few days. I had insisted that we should do the minimum in terms of intervention. Her hug told me that we had done the right thing. Just sitting beside her when she cried had opened the door for new life to begin.

After about two months, we wrapped up our work at the Lido Hotel although it was by no means finished. What happened to cause the tragedy remains a mystery. In July 2015, a piece of an airplane wing definitively linked to the aircraft by serial number was found on an island off the coast of Africa. Other small items have been found which are thought to be likely related.

A large percentage of the MH370 passengers' families subscribed to the conspiracy theories. There was little we could do to help them while they remained in that space, but we somehow managed to help as many people as we could, and we even helped a few to stop focusing on the theories and start rebuilding their lives.

As for what is the truth, I don't have the answer. Is it possible that the hard-core group was right about some of the conspiracies and cover-ups? I do not know. Our sole goal was to help people start to heal, to stand up, and begin to breathe again.

Conclusion

Shortly after I wrote my Letter to My Heart, I felt my health improving. With the aid of prayers, meditation, and intervention through traditional medicine, my condition miraculously stabilized.

As word got out of my improved health, I got a call from Mr. Spencer Fowler, the principal of Dalton Academy, an international school program at The Affiliated High School of Peking University. Mr. Fowler asked me if I could become a full-time teacher at the Academy.

Of all the career choices and titles available to me, the idea of being a teacher might not be considered a top choice. However, I remembered what I had written in my Letter to My Heart:

I would love share my path with others who seek a life with meaning. I want to inspire them and pass on the gift of giving; that would be a wonderful gift to the world.

When I took that into consideration, I realized that Dalton was just the place I needed to be. Dalton is a completely different high school compared to the typical Chinese high school. Just about all the students are destined to go study overseas for their higher education. It is a progressive hybrid program where some of the classes are in Chinese, and the other classes are taught completely in English.

The teachers create their own courses. Just like in college, students from different grade levels choose classes depending on their interests. Instead of training the students to be expert test-takers, at Dalton, students are encouraged to develop independent critical thinking, develop skill sets that fit their own interests and profile, and blossom into unique individuals. Students are self-organized and self-governing on campus, run their own businesses, and even develop and teach some of their own courses. David Ross,

CEO of Partnership for 21ˢᵗ Century Learning, has called Dalton "the most entrepreneurial school on the planet."

On September 1, 2016, a few days short of my 53ʳᵈ birthday, I became a full-time high school teacher for the first time. The first three months were extremely difficult, and I was on the verge of quitting on an almost daily basis. After each class, I was so exhausted that I had to put my head on the desk for a short nap. It seemed that all I did was eat, sleep, and teach. But I knew that this was what I was supposed to do. So far, I have taught Humanities, Psychology, Poetry, Screenplay Writing, and Music Appreciation. My heart has graciously grown accustomed to the workload as long as I am attentive and take rest when I need it.

The most magical class that happened was in the fall semester, 2017. During the previous semester, one of the students had done a study on teenage suicide. This student became concerned when his research pointed to the fact that teenagers who have emotional difficulties do not tend to speak to adults about it. She found that their close friends and fellow teens are the people who tend to notice first and have the best access to the teenager suffering emotional difficulties. When this concept was presented to the class, we had several engaging discussions. An idea emerged to create a class with the mission of designing a student-centered on-campus mental health program that is designed by students and run by students under the guidance of a mental health professional, who, in this case, was me.

I took on the responsibility of coordinating the class. I intentionally did not design every detail of the structure. I allowed the students to explore. They were extremely enthusiastic and wanted to become fully competent counselors!

After weeks of surveys, discussions, and research, the students came to realize that psychological counseling is very difficult work and should be left for professionals. What they decided upon, was that the best way to help fellow students would be to train some students with basic knowledge so that they could identify signs of potential problems. One of the most active students and the *defacto* leader of the class, Thomas, described this process as simply learning in a mindful, trained way, how to "be a better friend."

Psychology is now the most popular choice of college major for those who graduate from Dalton. This fact is interesting since I was told not too many years ago that "there was no place for psychology in China."

> *Psychology is now the most popular choice of college major for those who graduate from Dalton.*

Many of my friends and acquaintances have implored me to write a book about my experiences. My friend, Ken Rutt, was successful in inspiring me to make that a reality. As I was lying in my hospital bed after being given one week to live, I thought that, if by some miracle I was given the chance, I would write the book for Kimi. I wanted Kimi to know who her daddy was. However, I decided that this book shouldn't be about who I am. It should be about sharing with others what I have learned.

The true joy in life is not about winning. It is about helping others win. Your individual victories may bring about occasional sparks of pleasure and gratification, but true explosions of joy only happen when you are not only connected, but when you are of service to humanity and to the universe. It is only then that you can say, "The world is a better place because I was here."

Embrace the ocean.

Feel the explosions of joy.

ABOUT THE AUTHORS

Paul Yin was born in China and spent 22 years in the U.S. He returned to China to fulfill his dream of providing psychological service to his countrymen. Today, Paul is mostly known as a prominent psychologist from China. But he is a true renaissance man living a life of no-limits. On a unique winding path, and through events like the SARS epidemic, the Sichuan earthquake, Asiana Airlines Flight 214, and Malaysia Airlines Flight 370, he was guided into a life of answering the call of service to humanity. This is Paul Yin's debut publication in the U.S. He has published several books in China as well as numerous poems and magazine articles, and he has been a frequent guest on TV and radio.

Trina A. Kraus is a mom to two naughty cats named Lucky and Rudy along with two vivacious and intelligent little girls named Eden and Lily. She holds a Master's of Science in Education and has taught high school English for seventeen years in Pennsylvania and Washington. She is also a proud wife of a decorated U.S. Army veteran. Please visit her blog at www.trinaakraus.com to enjoy some tips from the heart of an English teacher who has cared deeply for her students and believes in making the world a better place through education.

CONTACT US:

VISIT WWW.EXPLOSIONSOFJOY.COM OR EMAIL
DIRECTLY TO AUTHORS@EXPLOSIONSOFJOY.COM TO
ARRANGE A SPEAKING ENGAGEMENT WITH PAUL YIN.

PAUL YIN IS AVAILABLE IN THE UNITED STATES:

JULY—AUGUST 2018

JANUARY—FEBRUARY 2019.

AVAILABLE INTERNATIONALLY BY REQUEST

68708152R00113

Made in the USA
Middletown, DE
31 March 2018